Vahur Laiapea

Diaries from Ukraine

Vahur Laiapea

DIARIES FROM UKRAINE

Bibliografische Information der Deutschen Nationalbibliothek
Die Deutsche Nationalbibliothek verzeichnet diese Publikation in der Deutschen Nationalbibliografie; detaillierte bibliografische Daten sind im Internet über http://dnb.d-nb.de abrufbar.

Bibliographic information published by the Deutsche Nationalbibliothek
The Deutsche Nationalbibliothek lists this publication in the Deutsche Nationalbibliografie; detailed bibliographic data are available on the Internet at http://dnb.d-nb.de.

Translated by Ott Palumäe and Tiiu Palumäe
Coverdesign by Jüri Kass
Foreword author: Vahur Laiapea, Jaanus Piirsalu

ISBN (Print): 978-3-8382-1977-6
ISBN (E-Book [PDF]): 978-3-8382-7977-0
© *ibidem*-Verlag, Hannover • Stuttgart 2025

Alle Rechte vorbehalten

Leuschnerstraße 40
30457 Hannover
info@ibidem.eu

Das Werk einschließlich aller seiner Teile ist urheberrechtlich geschützt. Jede Verwertung außerhalb der engen Grenzen des Urheberrechtsgesetzes ist ohne Zustimmung des Verlages unzulässig und strafbar. Dies gilt insbesondere für Vervielfältigungen, Übersetzungen, Mikroverfilmungen und elektronische Speicherformen sowie die Einspeicherung und Verarbeitung in elektronischen Systemen.

All rights reserved. No part of this publication may be reproduced, stored in or introduced into a retrieval system, or transmitted, in any form, or by any means (electronic, mechanical, photocopying, recording or otherwise) without the prior written permission of the publisher. Any person who commits any unauthorized act in relation to this publication may be liable to criminal prosecution and civil claims for damages.

Printed in the EU

Table of Contents

Our War in Ukraine 9

The Images and Smell of War in Ukraine 10

Saving Maria 13

Messages in the Morning and Evening 21

Ukrainians Are Like That 25

The Soldier's Two Graves 28

The Value of Chaplain Albert's Life 31

Responsibility For the Dead and the Living 36

Ruslan's Three Days of Torture 39

Izyum. Lost and Found 43

Potemkin's Bones and a Metre of Internet 46

Artem's Journey From Mariupol to Kherson 50

The Black Box Under Bakhmut 54

Volodomyr's Three Battles Under Bakhmut 57

Chaplain Dionissi's Service 59

Notes on Dead Villages 62

Deaths of Volunteers in Soledar 65

Lyman. The People Near War 69

Estonian Sauna and Half of a Mother's Heart 73

Pilots and Dead Bodies. The Free and The Bound 75

Cows and Butterflies in the Town of Kaminka 79

The Long Road to Becoming a Woman 83

A Love Letter from a Russian Prison 86

Ascension Day In Donbas 90

To Walk on Your Own Two Feet 93

Skeleton on a White Sheet 97

Sweet and Tender Beast 100

Wedding Gowns in the Kramatorsk Morgue 104

One Grave, Two Trenches 108

The Stunned People of Bakhmut 112

Cruel Jokes of War 115

Wagner Captives in Dnipro Prison 120

Anatoly's One Hundred Days of Torture 126

Auntie Lehte from Popilnia Village 130

The Liberation of the Azovstal Doctor 133

Estonian Body Armour and Bullets in Gunya's Body 137

Rubin's Remains From Izyum Forest 140

Fireworks in Mariupol and The Scorched Fields of Yaroslav 142

An Hour With a Prostitute 147

Water in Kherson and Afanasiivka 150

memory of him ever so calmly stating that seven out of sixteen soldiers had died still plays in my head.

There's a family with a disabled son living in Toretsk (another city in eastern Ukraine in the vicinity of battles that have been going on for months) in a five-story apartment building, the top two floors of which had collapsed during a missile strike. They live on the ground floor, the only family still living in that particular stairwell.

The mother holds her son, who is suffering from muscle atrophy, and says to him, "Oh God, how I love you!" They don't want to leave because they have nowhere to go. The son receives no aid, as there is no one to bring assistance. They live solely off love. This is my mental image of a mother's love.

No photo or video can truly capture the full brutality of the war in Ukraine. I have come to understand that the brutality of war often lies in those details that are difficult to convey. For example, war has a specific smell. It's a mixture of rotting flesh, dirt, urine, burnt things, and many other odours.

It seems to me that the best way to convey the brutality of the war in Ukraine is through the stories of ordinary people.

This is what Vahur Laiapea does with his stories. In addition, these accounts also answer the question of where Ukrainians find the strength to withstand all this brutality.

Jaanus Piirsalu
Journalist

The Images and Smell of War in Ukraine

I have some mental images from the war in Ukraine that keep coming back to me time and time again. They are not images of the dead, but of the living. Images of people living in the midst of indescribable brutality.

An older bearded woman in the basement of an apartment building in Chernihiv. She had been living in a dark basement for a month and a half. After the Russian forces had left and the bombings had stopped, it took another week before she dared to come out from underground. I first saw her in that basement a week after the war had started. She was a well-groomed older lady in nice clothes who spoke intelligently. The next time I saw her was in April. She had grown a sparse white beard, some longer strands up to ten centimetres long. She was wearing a dirty quilted jacket and her clothes had turned into rags. She smelled so bad that it was impossible to stand next to her. Her speech was so confusing that it made no sense to talk to her.

In a month and a half, constant bombings and the fear associated with it had turned the intelligent lady into a mad recluse. Her bearded and crazed face remains etched in my memory.

There's a Ukrainian officer I know near Avdiivka in Donetsk Oblast, where brutal battles had been raging for months. We drink coffee together at his command post and talk about what has happened in our lives in the meantime. He laughs as he talks about his life. Suddenly, a younger officer enters, calls him aside and tells him something. My acquaintance comes back and says that of the unit's sixteen soldiers who had gone out the day before, only nine returned. He resumes our conversation, laughing again after two minutes.

That was the moment I realised how calmly Ukrainian officers and soldiers accept death. Death is as common in their lives as coffee in the morning is to us. They all have accepted that any day could be their last.

The same officer was killed a month later. A shell had directly hit the bunker where he had been with three other fighters. The

Our War in Ukraine

The legend of the Holy Grail speaks of a paraplegic king. Parzifal did not ask a single question about the procession that was passing him. Nor did he ask about the woman carrying a vessel at the front of the procession. He saw but didn't ask. And because he failed to ask, women could not give birth, trees couldn't bear fruit, cows didn't give milk and the king became paralyzed. All because he had been taught to politely remain silent.

According to Russian writer Artur Solomonov, a priest from St. Petersburg has been arrested for claiming that Russian soldiers who die in Ukraine will not go straight to heaven. The paragraph under which he was charged deals with spreading false information about the army.

There can be various reasons for remaining silent. Comfort. Fear. Malice. Maybe it doesn't affect me. Maybe it will pass. Maybe someone else will deal with it.

It will affect us sooner or later. It won't pass if we don't intervene. We live in the vicinity of Russia, which is attacking Ukraine. We could be next. Or the ones after the next. It makes no difference. Our neighbour is a people who have lost their moral compass. A people whose chosen leaders have thoroughly trained them to hate us, prepared them to destroy us. Among them there are undoubtedly people who do not wish for this. But most of them remain silent. Maybe it will pass?

The texts in this book are written in Ukraine and Estonia between May 2022 and June 2023. In my written accounts I have tried to give a face to the people who continue to be ravaged by this hideous war.

Vahur Laiapea
In Suurupi on June 25, 2023

Saving Maria

Myhhail and Lyubov. Thirty-eight and thirty-eight. Workers at a factory in Mariupol, named Illichivsk. Lyubov is a crane operator, Myhhail a welder. Their daughter Maria is in her first year at Kharkiv University.

All three names have been changed. I don't take photos. Myhhail's mother and sister were left behind in Mariupol. His mother went insane due to the bombings, says Myhhail. He hopes to go back for them, to bring his mother and sister out of there. If they're still alive.

I'm used to listening. It always takes a lot of strength. Listening to Myhhail is hard. What he's experienced bursts out of him. He talks for three hours straight. Sometimes I can interrupt him and steer the conversation back to the "main theme". Stories have a way of branching out like apple tree branches. Sometimes they need to be pruned back.

Mariupol, the City of Maria. The Mother of God, after whom the Greeks arriving from Crimea named the city, hasn't been able to protect her city.

On March 10, 2022, Archbishop Sviatoslav Shevchuk, the leader of the Ukrainian Catholic Church, who visited Mariupol, said that Russian aggressors had turned the city into a graveyard. Two months later, it can no longer be called a graveyard. The dead are neither collected nor buried. They decompose in this onset of summer. Collecting the dead would cause too many new deaths.

Myhhail and Lyubov lived in the death-filled Mariupol until April 25. They made the decision to survive so that their daughter could survive. So that they could bring their daughter out of Kharkiv, where she lived under bombardment. We had a PLAN, says the father Myhhail. Death wasn't an option.

On February 24, Maria calls from Kharkiv. We're being bombed! As of February 24, work at the Illichivsk factory in Mariupol is still in full swing. Lyuba is sitting in the crane cab, Myhhail is welding. The city government reassures people: no need to panic.

The war will be over by Monday. No need to leave the city. On February 25, the factory is no longer functioning. The war won't be over by Monday. Not even by Tuesday. The war has only just begun. Only the VIPs could leave, Myhhail claims.

On March 2, the electricity in the city goes out. The same night, looters start raiding shops. Grocery stores are emptied. There is no water supply.

Myhhail and Lyubov live in a house in the factory district. The area is under constant bombardment. Tanks battle a hundred metres from their home. "When a tank fires a hundred metres away from you, the shock wave is so strong that you can't breathe," says Myhhail. Ahead lie two months of survival.

It's winter. There's a need for heat, water and food. There's a need to survive. There's a need to help neighbours, those single ladies next door as well. Neighbours also need water, firewood and food. How to gather all these things? Myhhail has a good bow saw. Almost every day, he goes to the park about a kilometre and a half away. In half an hour, he cuts down a tree, saws it into logs, loads the logs onto a cart, and brings them home. Then he goes back for more. The neighbours need firewood as well. The incoming missiles occasionally interrupt his sawing. Myhhail then lies down and waits. An explosion. He survives. He can continue working. Many people are cutting down trees in the park. Trees, damp trees, need to be split. For the neighbours as well. Only then can they be put in the stove. The room then becomes warmer and they can boil water over the stove to make tea. No water? Then you have to go to the river, where there's a spring. It's not like you can just go and collect water. There's a two-hour queue at the spring. Meanwhile rockets and shells are exploding in the vicinity. In eight weeks, there hasn't been a single trip during which missiles and shells haven't been exploding. The neighbours need water as well. Water needs to be fetched every day. You have to wash yourself, even if only as little as possible. One must maintain ritual hygiene habits to preserve human dignity. Survival is vital in order to ensure the rescue of their daughter.

How to bring the logs home? How to bring water? You need a cart for that. Where to get one? After a big air strike, you need to look for people who have died next to their cart. Myhhail goes. He needs a cart. There's a woman's corpse on the ground. Her hands and feet burnt. Next to the corpse is a cart. It is now available. It's now Myhhail's. He can bring home logs and water with it. The cart, at the meeting ground of life and death, becomes a means of survival. They're sold, exchanged. People are on the lookout for carts, as they can be exchanged for food.

The last of the food at home has run out. Myhhail and Lyubov ration one loaf of bread over two weeks. Where to get more food? They had preserves, but those have run out. Myhhail goes to search for food with a friend. They pass by a DNR (Donetsk People's Republic) unit checkpoint. There's a Ukrainian fighter's body displayed there, whose head and legs have been cut off. A scare tactic. Will they or won't they shoot? Will they kill or not? They don't shoot this time. Just search them.

PortCity, a large shopping centre, is located at the other end of the city. Of course, due to the bombings it's been out of operation for a long time, and looters have ransacked it. But also just regular people as well merely trying to find food, to survive. In the centre's culinary department, the men manage to find about 150 kg of cottage cheese, 150 kg of margarine, 100 kg of *povidl* plum jam, and some mayonnaise. They spend three days going back and forth under bombardment to collect all this food—for themselves and their neighbours. A total of 80 kilometres. They don't carry the food by hand, no one could do that. The men have bicycles, on which they hang the bags of food. They push the bicycles along.

Myhhail's mother and sister live in the same city near the central market. For weeks, their son doesn't know whether they're alive or not. He decides to go to his mother's house. He sees that it has been hit by a bomb. Myhhail doesn't dare to enter, afraid of finding his mother's and sister's corpses there. He goes back home. The next day, he decides to go and bury his loved ones. He asks a friend to come along. They reach the house. Mother! Mother! He enters. There's no one in the house—neither living nor dead.

The market square next to his mother's house. Nothing has been sold there for quite some time. There's a DNR separatist checkpoint there. In front of the checkpoint lies the body of a

Ukrainian fighter. His legs have been torn off by a bomb fragment. His stumps are tied up, he hasn't bled out right away. The man suffers for three days in front of the guards before God summons him.

The streets are used to transport the wounded, the invalids. When lacking better means, trash containers are used. For these too have wheels. At every checkpoint, men have to bare their skin — to prove they don't have any tattoos related to the Azov Battalion. Myhhail has a tattoo on his shoulder, but it's not found. It's not an Azov one. Nevertheless, every such discovery could mean death.

Where are his mother and sister? Coincidence provides the answer. Lyuba goes to an administrative office to get some kind of permit and happens to meet Myhhail's sister there. His sister, together with their mother, have taken refuge in a basement near the railway station. Their mother went insane according to the sister. Myhhail doesn't go to see them. He only takes trips that help him survive, in order to carry out THE PLAN. Water, firewood, food. Praying in the dark at home. Men disappear. If they're not killed, they're taken to a filtration camp. They're forced to fight for the DNR side.

On March 27, Myhhail meets two Ukrainian fighters in his backyard. Bohdan and Deniss. Young wide-eyed boys. He talks with 19-year-old Bohdan for five minutes. We came to protect you, says Bohdan. Two hours later a battle begins. Ten metres away from Myhhail and Lyuba's house. After the battle, Myhhail looks for traces of Bohdan and Deniss. There are no bodies to be found, no blood. Maybe they survived? Were they captured? Where are Bohdan and Deniss, the 19-year-old defenders of Ukraine?

Russian soldiers have a sense of humour. They stop Myhhail and his friend and aim their rifles at their knees. "Don't worry, you have two of them." Cheerful guys. Chechens aren't such great jokers. They open automatic fire above the heads of people standing right in front of them. They are skilled marksmen. No one gets shot, only one ear gets clipped. But the other one, of course, remains intact.

To save the daughter, in order to reach her, money is needed. Money is needed to buy gasoline for the car. The car is still in the yard, although the Chechens want to take it. They demand keys.

Myhhail refuses. Will they kill him? Not this time. They demand he hand over his motorcycle instead. He refuses. Will they kill him? Not this time. Without a car, Myhhail's PLAN would fail. Without a car, they would have no way to leave Mariupol.

There's no money. It must be found, earned. A bomb attack has "opened" the doors of garages. Myhhail enters them, looking for food. In one of them, he finds 5,000 hryvnia in a tin can. He doesn't take anything from the garages that he doesn't need. He finds some sugar, a jar of jam. He thanks the owner in his heart — what they have left behind will help his family survive. If he feels upon entering a garage that it doesn't feel right, he leaves it. He avoids becoming a marauder. Myhhail sells his and his wife's expensive bicycles. Someone buys their TV.

Myhhail and Lyubov were baptised a few decades ago. But the pendant crosses they received at their baptism ceremony have been misplaced, missing for fifteen years. Final preparations for the departure are underway. The crosses re-emerge. Myhhail puts his on, for Russian soldiers are God fearing people. The absence of a cross could have fatal consequences if, upon searching you, they discover that you're not wearing one. We've come to save you from the barbarians, Myhhail can already hear the Russian soldiers saying. Myhhail's neck bears the long lost cross to this day.

The morning of April 25. Departure from Mariupol. THE PLAN has been meticulously thought through, down to every last detail. What to say at the checkpoints? That we're moving to the neighbouring block, right nearby, of course. At the next one, say the same thing. Claim to be moving to a "new address" that's known and memorised by everyone in the car. In addition to Myhhail, there are five women in the car. Lyubov, a thirty-year-old woman, an eighteen-year-old girl, two more women from another family — a mother and daughter. Bags with personal belongings. The car's undercarriage is about to scrape the ground. But the tank is full of gasoline.

Mangush, a small town 20 km from Mariupol. Based on satellite photos, long traces of digging have been identified here which appeared at the end of March. Most likely mass graves. Graves of people killed in Mariupol. The time will come when everything becomes clearer. But Myhhail and his female travel companions don't know anything about these graves yet. They need to keep moving. You can't drive directly from Mariupol to the Russian border. That road could end in a filtration camp. The plan is to make it to Belgorod, near the Ukrainian border, by taking a long detour passing through Crimea into Russia. From there, crossing the border to Kharkiv to get Maria.

Berdiansk, Melitopol. A new cover story for the inspectors: I'm taking these people to Yalta, Crimea. Eleven hours pass by at the Crimean border crossing. Everything is searched. Someone in Berdiansk warned Myhhail that the border patrol uses a special program to identify when and how much information has been deleted from a phone. The phone's memory must not be "empty". Myhhail photographs random things, deletes what's necessary. The phone isn't "empty", doesn't arouse suspicion in the inspectors. You mustn't mention anything about the war at the border. That can get you brutally beaten. You have to say "special operation" instead. Passports are confiscated for ten hours. Six hours of waiting in an enclosure in one spot. There are stones underfoot that, even through shoe soles, begin to cause unbearable pain. Finally, they can drive on. Gasoline is running out. There's no money. Where to go and how?

In Dzhankoy, local Baptists give Myhhail the name of a contact who can help in Rostov-on-Don. The Kerch Bridge. Russia. Lukoil gas station. Electricity! Light! Warm water! The smell of hot dogs! The attendant shows mercy, allowing him to add 5 litres of gasoline to his tank free of charge. Mihhail is sitting in the car. What next? A woman approaches the car window, blue papers in her trembling hands. Russian rubles. She gives them to Myhhail. Two thousand rubles! The tank gets filled up. The driving can continue. Six hundred kilometres. Rostov-on-Don. Baptists take them in, take care of them, feed them. They can't eat too much at once, their stomachs have shrivelled. The hefty 110-kilogram Myhhail has become an 80-kilogram lean man. Warm water. A shower. Myhhail washes himself three times in a row. The baptists give Mihhail 5,000 rubles for his journey! That's a lot of money. It's 800 kilometres to Belgorod. Here too, the Baptists aid refugees. Caring and generous. Wealthy. The pastor of the congregation offers Myhhail money to help buy his daughter back from Ukrainian hands. As much as needed. "To buy her back? My daughter isn't in captivity. She doesn't need to be bought back," Myhhail says. "She needs to be extracted from the war zone."

By this time, Myhhail and Lyubov have managed to make contact with their daughter. The first time in over two months. Their daughter is still in Kharkiv. Myhhail isn't able to cross the border into Ukraine to get his daughter. The local pastor, to whom Myhhail is introduced, refuses to help him. His daughter is 90 kilometres away, but the road leading to her is blocked.

The generous pastor in Belgorod gives Myhhail 10,000 rubles. The journey to Smolensk begins. The Smolensk Baptists' pastor gives 20,000 rubles. THE PLAN has changed. Their daughter will have to be brought back through the Baltics and Poland. Myhhail and his family drive from Smolensk to the Pskov region, to the Estonian border. Nine hours of waiting in line. Estonian customs officers offer food.

On May 1, Lyubov takes an Estonian bus to Warsaw, and from there, a Ukrainian bus to Lviv. Maria has made her way to Lviv. On May 4, Lyubov and Maria arrive in Pärnu. Myhhail sees his daughter after over a year. THE PLAN has been executed.

But Myhhail and Lyubov send their daughter to Denmark a few days later. "Estonia is dangerous; it's not safe enough for her here. Russia is too close."

"To survive amid the bombs, there must be trees, a saw, water, bread, butter, a cart," Mihhail lists. And A PLAN, I add in my own thoughts, be it one of man or God.

Messages in the Morning and Evening

Niina and Halyna

Sahno village near Konotop. I enter an apartment building, which is home to Niina and Halyna. They are neighbours and friends. Their closely situated apartment doors have been in bad shape since the end of February, when Russians who occupied the village decided to stay in the building. Before they went on to free Kyiv. To conquer it.

The original residents fled to the cellar and slept there. Can we get some stuff from our apartment? The Russians are hospitable people. Overly hospitable even. Sure, you can. Go get your stuff and climb back to your cellar. The women then go to their homes, but their arms fall tiredly to their sides at the sight. In that short time their homes have been wrecked and dirtied. Room and cabinet doors have been ripped out and set in front of the windows. All their food has been eaten. Since February 26, the women may no longer go to their apartments.

There are animals in the barn. May I go feed the pigs? You may. A soldier with an automatic weapon will stand behind you, but you may.

Halyna had her son's clothes stored in a closet. Everything that caught someone's eye was taken. The soldiers have switched out their rubber boots for better ones. Dirty underwear lay on the floor. The Russian soldiers have found better and cleaner ones for themselves from a dresser.

Some of the soldiers love to talk. Vasja had come from a village close to Vladimir in Russia. "Why don't you have horses?" Vasja asks surprised. "Because we have tractors." "You live well here, your roads even have asphalt on them." Tolja from Orenburg consoles the ladies, "Don't worry, we'll take down your government. Then we'll live as we did before — as friends."

"And what did you do in Donetsk in 2014?" a Russian soldier exclaims. "Killed people!" "That wasn't all, we also ate local children," Niina answers. "That's where I got my belly fat from."

Niina is brave. She lets the Russian soldiers know all her thoughts on them. "Do they show our president on your television?" one of the soldiers asks. "They showed us that you prepared 400 000 body bags," Niina answers.

We go outside. I take photos. The residents start gathering clothes that Russian soldiers left behind after replacing theirs with better ones from Ukrainian homes. They come with a dirty shirt and three rubber boots. No underwear. Those were thrown away immediately.

Tamila

Right near Sahny village is Semjanivka. The villages have grown so close to each other, that only the locals know which house the next village starts from.

Tamila is seventy-one. A former teacher. Below her summer kitchen is a cellar, where she could fit more than ten people in addition to herself. The youngest of those being a four-year-old girl. Sonja. A brave girl. Didn't cry once. When it got quieter, people would sneak up from the cellar to the house for warmth. The gas heating still worked there. Back down again. This was in February, after all.

Tamila's house is by the main road in the village. Close proximity to the main road meant constant back and forth movement by Russian forces vehicles. There was endless fear over when they would come looting, or when they'd fire at the house from their automatic rifles or machine guns. A helicopter flew over the house. It stayed so low that Tamila could see the pilot's face. Will they shoot? The pilot even smiled at her. Friendly people.

Kadyrovians. Those were the scariest. You never knew when they would shoot at your windows. They riddled one of my student's sons' legs with bullets when he crossed paths with them while driving near a bridge in his car. He managed to crawl under the bridge. He was saved. He's alive.

Tamila grew up just as was common in those times of the Soviet enslaved people's union. Young Pioneer. Young Communist. School. The institute. Belief in what they fed the soul. She became a

Ukrainian language and literature teacher. Somewhere deep inside her soul a BIG CHANGE was in waiting, her spiritual awakening. That time came. Everything changed, opened up, got new meaning. "We changed tremendously," Tamila says.

An ordinary story. Relations with relatives living in Samara, Russia have ceased, ties have been severed. They grew distant back in 2014. "They invite us to live with them in Russia, away from the war. Here they kill us, yet invite us to Russia? Here I can say whatever I think out loud. I live in a free country. Go to Russia?"

Tamila recalls a message written on a wall in Bucha by Russian soldiers. She saw it on social media. WHO ALLOWED YOU TO LIVE BETTER LIVES THAN US.

"Envy is behind all of this," Tamila says.

Julia

Julia's house by the main road has been severely damaged. She now lives in the summer kitchen in the yard with her two children. Her daughter is eight, and her son is six. Julia's grandmother also lived there in the first months of the war, before the attack on her house.

Julia's husband is a career soldier. When the war broke out, he was at home. On the same day, he was called to Konotop. She saw her husband again only in April. She finds out that Anatoli had taken part in the freeing of Bucha. Right now, he is fighting in Donbas. They've agreed that he will send her two messages a day. One in the morning, the other in the evening.

The Russian army made its way to the bordering towns very quickly. On February 25, the street was filled with their war materiel. People from the neighbouring regions created a social group on the Telegram platform, where they would share intel with each other on the movements and behaviour of the Russian forces. It was important to know when to be ready to take cover, and when there was a little bit of time to take a breath.

On April 1, Julia got a message from her friend on Telegram, that a retreating and very aggressive Russian unit was approaching their village. The unit reaches their street. Soldiers sit on top of tanks and other machines. They can't fit inside because they've stuffed them full of stolen goods. It's time to hide in the cellars. Julia's grandmother refuses to go into the cellar. She stays in the house. Julia asks her to stay in the room she finds to be the safest. A big explosion. Julia looks out of the cellar window from next door. We don't have a home anymore, she tells her mother on the phone. But grandma, is she still there? Julia pulls herself together and goes into the wrecked house. Grandma's not in the room where Julia asked her to stay. She had gone to her room right before the shooting. The only one which stayed intact, more or less. She went there for two reasons. She had to charge her phone. And she went to pray in her icon corner.

Julia was convinced—someone gave the Russians the information, that the family of a Ukrainian soldier lives in this house. It was the only house in the village that the Russians fired a close range direct hit at. They shot at it with an RPG, a weapon meant to destroy tanks.

I start to make my way out. I spot an old suitcase with metal corners by the wall. "Here are grandmother's burial clothes," says Julia. She opens the suitcase. "See, these types of shawls are tied around the heads of our deceased women." She closes the dust-covered suitcase. Right now grandma is at her daughter's place, Julia's mother's home in a neighbouring village. Julia takes care of the kids. She waits for the evening message from her husband.

Ukrainians Are Like That

Ljuba met Estonians for the first time in 1987 as a nineteen-year-old girl. A married couple from Estonia came to visit their family. The husband was called Jaan. The woman? Well, a name is just a name. The woman wore a beautiful full-length crimplene dress. Tailored to fit her body. With ruffles. How beautiful it was! To this day, Ljuba associates Estonia with that woman and her dress. Oh, how she would have wanted a dress just like that one.

Serhii is known worldwide for his brave act, but few know his name. He is the man that millions of people saw on television and on social media in February 2022. He is the man who stopped a Russian tank with his bare hands at the beginning of the war. He stood in front of the tank. He kneeled down in front of it. "Go ahead, run me over, but I won't move." The only weapon he had at hand was his bicycle. He had already thrown it at the tank. And at another one. The tanks ran over it. The remains of the bicycle were left behind, scattered about the city square. Afterwards, his friends raised some money and gave him a new one.

All of this happened in the city of Bakhmach on February 26. All the news channels were talking about this man who went against a Russian tank with his bare hands and held it back. They all showed the video of him. But nowhere has the name of this brave man, whose deed had touched the hearts of so many people, been mentioned.

A good companion with knowledge regarding local life is very important on trips like these. Dmytro and I have been travelling together for ten days. With his help, we've reached people I couldn't reach alone. My goal for our last day working together is to find the man who stopped the tank. We don't know his name nor his address. We only know that he did it in the city of Bakhmach. That's exactly where we're headed from Konotop. People on the streets, at church, at the police station, everyone knows that such a man exists, but nothing more. A woman stands near an apartment building, holding an embroidered Ukrainian ethnic shirt. I ask her if it's for sale. It is not. We ask about the man who stood in front of the tank. The woman takes out her phone and makes five calls to her acquaintances. She gives them the task of finding out who this man is and where he lives. Their efforts bear fruit. One person can provide us with an address. We are very grateful to the woman for helping us. And what does she do? She gives me the embroidered ethnic shirt which was made in the Carpathians. Not a penny! Ukrainians are like that.

We drive to the address we were given. A street lined with lilacs in bloom. The man isn't at the address. There isn't even a house at the address. This here is Decembrists Street. Serhii doesn't live on Decembrists Street. A rescue worker passing by comes to our aid. He makes a phone call. Asks us to wait. Drives away. Comes back half an hour later and tells us to follow him. He takes us to a young man who can guide us to our hero. And so he does. Ukrainians are like that.

Serhii and Ljuba are surprised but not alarmed. They laugh joyfully. "How did you find us?" No journalists have visited them so far.

How did it all happen? Serhii admits that he didn't have his wife's permission to go to the city square. He apparently kept quiet about what had happened when he got home as well. Ljuba only found out about it when the godmother of her children called her. "Turn on the TV! Serhii's on there!"

Serhii Sevtchenko. Fifty-seven years old. A former Soviet army tank commander named Sergei Sevtchenko. He served in Hungary in 1986. That year marked thirty years since the anti-Soviet uprising in Hungary. Battle readiness. Everything remained calm, there was no need to drive over people with tanks. "They didn't like us there," says Serhii. "Our guys used to go into people's gardens to steal fruit. We wanted something fresh. Vitamins."

When a former Soviet tank commander who has become a Ukrainian patriot steps in front of a Russian tank, he knows exactly where the tank driver's viewport is. "That's what I blocked with my body," says Serhii. Without seeing anything, he couldn't drive any further.

Serhii brings out his old tank commander's cap from the back room. He puts it on. It doesn't fit very well. He pulls it on anyway.

He talks about what and how you hear while driving a tank. What muffles the noise and how to convey orders.

When I'm about halfway through filming and listening to Serhii, something changes in him. The brave man falls silent mid-sentence. His eyes fill with tears. We remain silent for a long time, and then he continues.

The story being told by Serhii Sevtchenko, the former Soviet tank commander, was cut short when he tried to express how great his concern for his country and people is. How important this land and these people are to him. Ukrainians are like that.

The Soldier's Two Graves

In the summer of 2021, Halyna stood in her yard. Clap! A sniper's bullet penetrated a wall of the house a few dozen centimetres above his head. It was a warning shot, Halyna thinks. The game. If they wanted to kill me, they would have done it. The previous owner of the house was killed by separatists just outside the door of the home in 2014. The bullet penetrated the heart, the scare games were not played. The house was empty and the owner's loved ones gave it to Yevheny and Halyna to live in. During eight years of war, a dozen people in the village were killed by snipers. These were, of course, not the only casualties of war in this village.

Chermalyk is the name of this village. It is located in the Donetsk Oblast, 40 km from Mariupol on the Kalmius River. After the great battles of 2014 and 2015 in the region, the river remained a dividing line between the occupiers and the positions of the Ukrainian army. In Mariupol, the river flows into the Sea of Azov. Yevheny and Halyna lived in the most riverside and most dangerously located house in the village of Chermalyk from 2015 to February 24 of this year.

In every person's life, there comes a time when God knocks at the door of their heart. So says Yevheny, a 62-year-old Ukrainian army chaplain.

Yevheny and Halyna found faith together in February of 2000. Together they became chaplains in the Ukrainian army around 2015. Together they have lived and performed their chaplain work right on the front lines for seven years. The war did not leave the area. They were also on the front lines without leaving their homes. Every step out of the house, every move in the courtyard could result in death.

Death is the beginning of new life, says Yevheny. Life is eternal. These are the convictions he has shared with many people as chaplain. In early May of 2017, a minivan with Ukrainian soldiers hit a mine just outside the front line. The remains of the soldiers were sent to their families for burial. Some time later in the same place, fellow fighters found remains that had not been sent home nor buried. Parts of the body and items of one fighter—Olyksandr. Some of him had already been sent home. The soldiers wanted to bury the remains there at the place of death, to hold a service at the grave, to erect a cross bearing the name of the fighter. Yevheny handed over the car keys to Halyna. Under Grad fire and accompanied by a couple of soldiers, he went to bury the remains of the fallen soldier. This was one of the few cases where the commander of the unit wouldn't allow Halyna to go along. Halyna took the keys and waited with the knowledge that the possibility of her husband being killed was very high. Forty minutes later, the burial men got back. "We prayed in whispers," Yevheny told his wife. "The enemy was so close that they could have heard us." This is how the unknown Olyksandr has two graves in Ukraine—in his home cemetery and in the territory currently occupied by the Russians. Does the cross bearing his name still stand?

In 2015, there were many people in the village of Chermalyk who were waiting for the separatists to come and provided them with information. Perhaps even half of the one thousand five hundred or so inhabitants were pro-Russian, Yevheny thinks. There were topics we never talked about over the years. In their church and missionary work, the chaplain couple did not distinguish between pro-Ukrainian and pro-Russian people. When humanitarian aid was distributed, people from both camps stood in the same queue. Went to the same church. And, of course, everyone knew who belonged where.

What do the soldiers tell the chaplain? What's weighing on the heart? A sniper asks if God forgives him for killing people. "Differentiate between murder and protecting your own," the chaplain answers him. "They came to kill us and our loved ones. Only we can protect them from this." A drunken villager stumbles over from the separatist side to the Ukrainian side in the dark. Soldiers at the guard post give the order to stop. They fire a warning shot in the air. The response is profanity. The guard shoots. The drunk dies. The heart is plagued. Prayer with the chaplain. The watchman's heavy heart is relieved.

Around February 20, a heavier-than-usual bombardment began from enemy positions. Well, they'll bang a little and calm down, thought Yevheny. It didn't calm down. A lot happened on February 24. In the morning, the two chaplains drove under fire from Grad rockets to the village of Orlovskoye to hold a service. Three people came to the service. Then they had to go to Mariupol to fix a car tire. On the way, they saw a couple of dozen Russian tanks on fire. The tire was repaired. Back to the village. Yevheny still hoped it would "become quieter." That the war would stay in place. No. The big war was on the move. Back to Mariupol. The Russian invaders were encircling the city. On February 25, Yevheny and Halyna, together with a convoy of twenty cars and buses, arrived in western Ukraine. It was led by a special team of the Ukrainian army. Russian tanks were seen on the way. They were going as fast as 160 km/h at times. They drove for their lives, or rather, away from their deaths.

Western Ukraine. Yevheny is itching to return to the front. You can't get into Mariupol anymore. He reaches Zaporizhzhia. His health is failing. His legs that have been struggling and in pain for a long time need peace and healing. He goes back. Together with Halyna and their daughter Polina, who made it to the border, they arrive in Estonia. An old friend, Pastor Artur Põld, takes them into his care.

The Value of Chaplain Albert's Life

Albert Homjak knows the value of his life. The Russians pay three thousand American dollars for every chaplain killed. Perhaps even more by now. As the war continues, the price could increase. Albert has been on the list of people to be shot in Mariupol since 2014. If the occupiers get their hands on him, that will be that. He has the honour of being at the top of that list, not at the bottom. In reality, no one knows the price of chaplain Albert.

During our five-hour meeting, Albert checks his phone after every notification. He is the commander of the military's chaplain's battalion in Zaporizhzhia. All information about what's going on trickles down to his phone. He continues to coordinate the work of the chaplains from Estonia. Albert came to Estonia from Ukraine to rest for a week. He brought his responsibilities with him for this week.

After lunch, Albert and I walk towards his room. From a distance, a boy runs towards us. He jumps and hugs Albert. This is how you hug a father if you have a father to love. Not everyone has one. 56-year-old Albert has never seen his own father and doesn't even know who his father was. Albert has nineteen sons and one daughter. He doesn't have any biological children; they are all taken under care. He took in his first child in 2000, and the most recent a couple of years ago. Adoption isn't practical because it would disqualify him from the albeit meagre support provided by the state for raising children as a foster parent. A father is a father when he is a father. A paper doesn't make anyone a father. Albert is a father.

Since 2012, Albert has been working at the Mariupol Pilgrim orphanage—more precisely, it's a shelter and rehabilitation centre. It's an independent, donation-based organisation with a religious background, founded and led to this day by Mariupol's legendary pastor Gennadi Mohnenko. In the 1990s, he began working with street children. Over time, it has become a well-functioning network through which thousands of homeless children have been rescued and given a new life. A Google search brings up "Pilgrim Republic Children's Home" as one of its names. It's not just an orphanage but a whole network of rehabilitation services for anyone in need, including adults whose lives have gone awry. The children of the Pilgrim Republic Children's safehouse were evacuated away from the Russian attacks to Zaporizhzhia. Who is a pilgrim? A pilgrim is a person who is on a journey to a holy place. In Mariupol, tens of thousands have now set out on a journey—some to heaven, some to find a safe place on earth. And yet the Russians still claim in international forums that girls are being trained as snipers and boys as throat-cutters at Pilgrim Republic. Of course, for the purpose of killing Russians. The pastor in charge, Mohnenko, is ahead of Albert on the hit list.

Thirteen-year-old Vanja, who jumped into Albert's arms, joined his family from the Pilgrim home a couple of years ago. He is the youngest of the children. Six of Albert's sons are in the war. In the five hours that we spoke I didn't get down all the doings of all of his sons. I managed, however, to hear a bit more about the fate of some of them.

Vanja, like Albert's other sons, is under guardianship, not adopted. This means that if there are people willing to adopt him into their family, it's possible to do so with the child's consent. After Vanja had lived with Albert's family for some time, a mother and daughter appeared who expressed a desire to adopt the boy. At that time, 11-year-old Vanja decided to give it a try. A month and a half later, Albert's phone rang in the middle of the night. It was the mother and daughter. Take this boy away from us, or we'll send him to an orphanage. Albert brought Vanja back home. Vanja hasn't talked about what happened or why the woman gave up on him. Albert attributes it to their background, their trauma. The two women's son and brother died in the war in 2015. Presumably, the mother and sister—both teachers by profession—wanted to find a son for their family who would serve as a replacement for the deceased son, filling the void left behind. This is a poor starting point for adoption, according to Albert. Vanja didn't meet the women's expectations, Albert believes.

Six of Albert's sons are in the army, five of them on the front lines: Dima, Misha, Vova, Kolya, David. Since 2019, David had been serving in the Mariupol navy, on a boat. He was the cook and machine gunner on the boat. When the Russians started their offensive towards Mariupol, the unit came ashore to defend the city. David remained in the city for forty days after it was occupied, hiding. He couldn't leave, or rather, couldn't attempt to leave until all traces of wearing a heavy bulletproof vest around his neck had disappeared. And until the faint traces of gunpowder and gun oil on his right thumb and index finger had faded. I can't describe the details and techniques David used to leave the city — they are still used to rescue people today. At the last checkpoint before leaving the city, a Russian soldier demanded that David show his right thumb and index finger. The trained eye of a professional soldier would immediately spot the gunpowder residue. David's escort found a way to divert the Russian soldier's attention away from David's hand. What he did remains a secret. The young man got away. He is back in service, now in northern Ukraine.

What does a chaplain do? Everything that life requires of him. When needed, he carries the wounded, tends to their wounds, listens, gives encouragement, prays. After the occupation of Mariupol, Albert has been involved in evacuating people who have remained in villages near the front line. These are villages, the residents of which are often under fire. Mostly elderly people who didn't want to leave their homes but whose lives are now placed in serious danger. Rescuers often fall under fire. Animals frequently give warning signs several minutes before shelling begins. Once in Shyrokyne, a pack of dogs ran past Albert and left the village. Five minutes later, mines began falling on the village. Geese become nervous and start honking before an incoming attack. Geese once saved Rome from the conquerors of Gaul — how else other than by honking.

The evening approaches. I take pictures of Albert. He changes from his Mariupol Pilgrim shirt into his chaplainS's shirt. On one shoulder, there are golden words written in black ink — "Slaves to sin are not allowed into paradise." I think to myself — neither, probably, are slaves of any other kind.

Albert has a cat at his home in Ukraine. When he goes outside, he lets the cat roam freely. Recently, Albert went to Finland. He took the cat with him. In Finland, there is a law that doesn't allow cats to roam freely on the streets. They must be on a leash. Albert put a leash on his cat in Finland. In response, the cat lay down in the street and refused to move any further. It had the freedom to choose. If Russians living in Russia can't say what they think about the invasion of Ukraine and about the killing of Ukrainian people, then they can at least remain silent. Not endorse it. That freedom they do have, says Albert. Like the cat that lay down on the street. Such metaphors for slavery and freedom.

How did Albert find his faith? Through colonies and prisons where he spent a total of twelve years as a boy and a young man. His crimes — thefts and robberies to obtain drugs. He wast last sentenced to prison in 1994. A friend invited Albert to the prison's church, telling him that God could fulfil his wishes. Albert thought that only those inmates who had fallen very low, those on the lowest rung of the inmate hierarchy, went to the prison's church. He didn't go. Albert said that if he were to be released early, he would go to church. He knew there was no hope for an early release. He had already accumulated too many convictions.

One fellow inmate worked in the prison office. He processed documents for those eligible for amnesty. There were the names of twenty-three prisoners on the list. He accidentally added a twenty-fourth line to which there was no name to add. The judge didn't count the names but relied on the number on the paper. He decided to release **twenty-four** prisoners early. The inmate working in the office added Albert's name as the twenty-fourth to cover up his mistake. Albert was released three years ahead of his release date.

Freedom and a promise waiting to be fulfilled — going to church. A promise must be kept. He went to an Orthodox church where he wanted to confess. The priest kicked him out. Albert — what kind of a name is that? Go find out your true baptismal name. Albert went to a newly opened Protestant church. Went there with doubt, not faith. He had heard that Protestant churches were established with U.S. support and intended for espionage. He went with the intention of deceiving the enemy. To steal from them. To gain an advantage. He went, went again, and kept going. He didn't steal. He was freed from slavery. He truly became free. Only people who are free enter paradise, not slaves. He put the shirt with the message on for the photo.

"Our first duty as Christians is to give children the opportunity to hug their mother and father in the morning. Either their mother or father. A mere caretaker or caregiver is not enough," Albert said at the beginning of our meeting.

In 2000, a boy came to the Christian club where Albert worked and asked, "Can I start living with you? My own family isn't good. Can I call you Dad?" Today, that boy, Albert's first child, is 36 years old. Jura lives with his family in Finland. He has a daughter. The daughter has a mother and a father.

Responsibility For the Dead and the Living

Andrei

Andrei has not slept for six years now. He dozes off, wakes up in the night, can't fall back asleep. Alcohol seems to be his daily painkiller. When I met him the other night, he was drunk. He remains anonymous in this story. I don't exist, says Andrei. I no longer have psychology, i.e. a psyche.

Andrei is a pathoanatomist who has been working in the Kharkiv morgue for six years already. Not only in the morgue — he uses his phone to show me pictures of the dead lining the streets, from where he retrieved bodies while under fire from the Russian occupiers back in March and April already. Bodies or pieces of them. You can't show these photos in public.

We meet outside the morgue on Dmytrivska Street in Kharkiv. There are black plastic bags lying right there on the asphalt. Not empty bags. Each one contains a human corpse. Judging by the shape of some bags, you can guess that there are just pieces of a human body. You're not allowed to take pictures there, but I still snap a couple. It's not a war secret that people die in it. The bus marked Cargo 200 backs up to a tent at the entrance of the morgue. A corpse is carried in on a stretcher. Covered with a sheet, there's an arm hanging over the stretcher's edge. An arm without a hand. Greyish blue.

Ukrainian soldiers stand on the street in front of the morgue. They smoke. They wait. There are a couple of artificial wreaths in their cars. The soldiers have come to pick up their fallen comrade and are going to send him off.

Andrei is hungover, aggressive. He interrogates me and is hostile. I don't get offended. He's as broken as can be. "Ukraine should close all borders and impose the death penalty. Anyone caught guilty of corruption must be shot. NATO dares not do anything if Russia were to use a nuclear weapon." Those are his views. Andrei needs help, but he's really not ready to accept any. Not yet. We part ways.

Pavel

Pavel is a doctor who worked in Balaklia throughout the occupation. Many colleagues left. Pavel is a critical care doctor and anesthesiologist.

On February 24, he wakes up in his home exactly one minute before the war begins. A minute before the first explosions are heard. He knew the war was coming. He had received information the previous night that all cell phones had been collected from Russian soldiers.

On February 26, Pavel goes to work — to the hospital. The hospital is located in a forest near the city. Soon after the occupation began, wounded Russian soldiers were brought there. In early March, a nineteen-year-old young man is brought in. He's got a brain injury, paralyzed right side. He's conscious. His kidneys and liver are badly damaged. Ukrainian doctors try to save him, but the soldier boy dies. "I stood there and pondered," says Pavel. "A nineteen-year-old boy. He has a mother somewhere. What's all this for?"

In March, the occupiers kill Pavel's colleague, a nurse. His son was just born, and he's on his way home from getting some nappies for the baby. The medic has his fingers cut off, his knees shot, his face badly beaten. Finally, he's killed with a "mercy shot" to the head.

The hospital is under Russian control. Fear. Terror. The Russians make the chief doctor sit on the stairs and shoot him between the legs. No real harm, the shot is a scare tactic. On April 3, all staff are ordered to gather in the hall. Masked soldiers carrying automatics surround them. No communication, no explanation. Pavel's afraid they'll all be shot. "They were fascists — they were the same as how I had imagined German fascists to be," says Pavel. A Russian officer — probably an FSB employee — gives a speech to the staff. "The hospital needs to continue its work. We came here to destroy the fascists and nationalists of Ukraine. There are many of them, especially among young people."

On April 4, the hospital is hit by a bomb and stops functioning. Pavel and a few other employees continue to work at the city's outpatient clinic. Pavel lives at the clinic. He doesn't move around in the city. One of the hospital's surgeons, Irina, continues to work alongside him at the clinic. They can trust each other.

People who have been tortured by the occupiers are brought to the clinic, which at this point also functions as a hospital. Anything of value had apparently been beaten out of them. None are taken back—apart from one. There are traces of electric torture on their bodies. These beaten men were like frightened children, says Pavel. Humble and obedient. One of the prisoners brought to the hospital is dying. Pavel wants to give him morphine. He is, however, still taken to Kupyansk Hospital. The man dies there. His body was deformed by beatings, bruised from head to toe. Blisters covering both hands up to his elbows. Probably poured over with some kind of liquid. Boiling water, maybe? Tears pour into Pavel's eyes. He apologises and steps away for a minute or two.

Pavel did not visit his home village during the entire occupation period. He lived and worked at the hospital. Still lives and works there to this day. "I didn't do anything special," says Pavel. "My suffering was not that extensive."

His mother and two dogs stayed behind. One of the dogs died. His name was Tsar. Tsar was Pavel's favourite dog. I really missed the dogs, says Pavel. I missed them more than I did the people.

Ruslan's Three Days of Torture

Ruslan is a 47-year-old former ATO soldier. ATO is short for three words: "Anti-Terrorist Operation". This is the official term that was used in 2014 to describe the war initiated by Russia, in which it supported separatist movements against Ukraine. I met Ruslan at his home in Izyum.

On the morning of August 24, 2022, two men came to Ruslan's house. Bogatyr and another man whose nickname Ruslan doesn't remember. "We have information that you're a nationalist," they told Ruslan. They searched Ruslan's house, blindfolded him, and took him away. Ruslan believes he was taken to the White House, as he refers to the building that served as the Russian military headquarters. Cars were switched once during transportation. While being kidnapped, he could hear the flowing of a river and the smell of gasoline. There was probably a gas station nearby. These were the only signs he could perceive. Ruslan's hands and feet were tied together with a short piece of rope, leaving him in a crouched position.

He remained in this position for three days. For three days Ruslan's eyes were covered. At 3 p.m. on August 24, the interrogation began. Ruslan didn't deny that he had served in the Ukrainian armed forces from 2015 to 2017. "Who else do you know from the ATO? Where are the families of the soldiers? And the families of the police officers?" I don't know any names, everyone has left. The torture began, lasting six hours. Ruslan was stripped naked. He was tortured with a shock baton, a specialised device for electric torture. Ruslan was made to stand on a metal surface through which the torturers administered electric shocks. Then to the basement. No food was given. Actually, no — once, during the three days, his tormentors did give Ruslan a small piece of bread sprinkled with sugar. He forced himself to eat it to avoid getting beaten for refusing. He was taken to the toilet once during those three days. That, of course, wasn't enough.

On August 25, the interrogators came to the basement. Beating ensued. In the face, the body. The beatings took place periodically, with breaks. A total of four times. Even beaters need rest. Ruslan's hands and feet were tied, bending his body.

August 26. "We're going to kill you," say the torturers. "Say your goodbyes to your loved ones in your mind." Ruslan is put in a car. Driven somewhere. Taken out of the car. Pushed from behind. Ruslan tumbles down a steep slope. His hands and feet are still tied, but the rope connecting the two is removed. His eyes are covered. "You can remove the blindfold in five minutes," they say.

Ruslan counts, trying to keep track of time. He removes the blindfold with bound hands. He sees the golden domes of Izyum's church in the distance. He gets a rough idea of where he is. He manages to free his hands and feet. Instead of going straight home, he goes to his parents' house nearby. His mother starts crying. She cleans her son's wounds, treats his bruises and swollen areas with oil. Ruslan eats a little and falls asleep. His wife comes to pick him up in a taxi.

Ruslan doesn't leave his home for two weeks. He eats little and sleeps a lot. Then he goes back to work. He works for a sewage company. On September 9, the liberation of Izyum begins. On September 10, Ukrainian forces enter the city. Ruslan's wife retrieves a hidden Ukrainian flag symbolising the struggle for freedom from its hiding place and hangs it outside their house.

If Ruslan had been captured in the early months of the occupation, he probably wouldn't have been left alive. Such is his fate. "I think I was beaten lightly," Ruslan says. "The physical pain was bearable. The emotional pain was much greater. Will I continue fighting? If need be. Although true, I am in poor health."

Russian occupiers search, torture, and kill ATO soldiers wherever they can. Not just them, of course. They've been doing it since February 24. On the outskirts of Izyum, there's a beautiful pine forest. Mushroom foragers have already been spotted there. There lie the defensive lines of the Russians, with bunkers and trenches, right next to the graves of the people they've killed. Shallow graves, barely a metre deep, are now empty. The bodies have been dug up in the past few weeks and taken to morgues for identification. From some graves, an empty coffin stares out, with the deceased removed. Some contain rags. Empty food cans. Wooden crosses bear numbers for the most part. Three hundred and twenty. Three hundred and twenty-six. Some have the name of the deceased, date of birth and death. Some even have an address. A few graves have memorial plaques. One reads: *Here rests Leonov, Vitali Sergeevich. 29.05.1980 – 14.05.2022. Eternal remembrance.* The grave number is three hundred and twenty-nine.

Daniil Prokopenko was killed on May 4. On June 13, he would have turned twenty. At the bottom of the grave lies an opened coffin. Daniil's body has been taken to the morgue for an autopsy. One day, this young man who remained nineteen, will have a new resting place, a new coffin, and a new cross at his burial site. Eternal remembrance.

The smell of death lingers in the forest. Still.

Izyum. Lost and Found

Yesterday was a strange day. In the morning I meet a Ukrainian paramedic named Olyksandr at the Kharkiv Hotel. A week ago, he drove to villages near Staryi Saltiv, and retrieved two killed Ukrainian fighters. He mentioned the village of Khotimlia, also the bridge over the Seversky Donetsk River that was destroyed at the beginning of the war. It was bombed to pieces by Ukrainian forces in order to keep the occupiers from moving on to Kharkiv. Crossing the bridge, one could get to Kharkiv in half an hour.

These soldiers had gone to a village in the newly liberated territory to determine whether all the Russians had left. They saw people on the street wearing a mix of civilian clothes and Russian military clothing. "Oh, hello! Finally, the Ukrainians—the liberators. How we have been waiting for you!" The villagers invited the Ukrainian soldiers into a house where Russian occupiers were waiting. They captured the Ukrainian soldiers, shot through their knees and slashed open their stomachs.

A few days ago, I accompanied young men who were organising humanitarian aid to the villages there. I don't know if we went to the village where the aforementioned happened. Maybe. I just had this image in my mind of how the same villagers who led the Ukrainian soldiers to their deaths were now accepting humanitarian aid. And dozens of organisations are now giving aid to the newly liberated villages.

It's my last day working in Kharkiv. We go to Izyum for the third time with Seryozha, my *fixer*. We have information about two people whose loved ones are missing. They heard that an Estonian journalist had been to Izyum and hoped that I could help find their missing loved ones with my work.

Natasha

On April 28, Russian soldiers came to Natasha's house and took her 31-year-old son with them. She hasn't seen her son since. The son, Yuri, was not involved in the army, police, or territorial defence.

Natasha heard a rumour that her son had been seen digging trenches for the Russians. She hasn't been able to confirm it. Another rumour is that the son has been seen on his way to Slovyansk. The last rumour circulated about a month ago — some man who had been sold by the Russians as a slave to a farm near Donetsk was said to have been released and returned to Izyum. He was said to have worked there with Yuri. Yuri was not released. They had worked in a barn taking care of the cows. Natasha has never met the guy who got free.

There's hope in Natasha's eyes. "I pray for my son every day. I pray that my son has the strength and health to return home." Natasha gets her son's passport from inside. I promise her I'll circulate the picture from her son's passport. Maybe people with relatives in Donetsk will see it who can ask around for a young man named Yuri Litvinov. Who then maybe discover that Yuri is alive, that maybe he's a slave on some farm and is in one piece. How much easier it would be for his mother Natasha if her hopes were confirmed.

Niina

Niina's husband Nikolai was born in 1948. On April 28, 2022, Nikolai sat on his Ukrainian bike and began pedalling towards the village of Kunye, which is thirty-five kilometres away. His bees live in Kunye village. Thirty beehives. He was going to go take care of them. Nikolai didn't make it there. His body has not been found. There's been no word of him making it to Kunye village.

Nina is hopeful. She's heard through a number of people that her husband had called his goddaughter, Alexandra, who lives in the village of Ternovaya, near Kharkiv. "I'm going away. Take care of the bees for me. I'll be back in two months," Nikolai had told Alexandra.

Nina and Nikolai's yard is very beautiful, very clean. Have you been to Estonia? "I have. We drove there by car in 2002. You know what struck me — how well kept and clean your graveyards are! I brought back three kringles from Estonia."

Seryozha and Izyum

We buy a piece of ham and some bread from the Izyum market. We eat. Then start to drive off. My assistant Seryozha sees a little dog on the side of the road. A puppy, we think at first. Shall we take it with us? Let's offer the dog at checkpoints — maybe Ukrainian soldiers will want to care for him. Seryozha stops the car. I get a piece of ham and a bottle of water from my bag. Seryozha feeds the dog and gives it water. Puts him in the back seat. We keep driving. At the first checkpoint, we offer the dog to the soldiers. "No, what are we going to do with him here?" At the second — "No, we don't want him." We keep driving. "I'll take him to my house at first," says Seryozha, who already has one rescued dog at home. I'm sure one of the residents will take him. What shall we name the dog? Izyum? Izyum, naturally.

We get to Kharkiv. We stop by Seryozha's home. He, at first, puts the dog in a basement room with windows. Gives him the last piece of ham and pours some drinking water. Izyum, found in Izyum, will definitely find a home, he won't be left on the streets. I'm absolutely sure of that.

Potemkin's Bones and a Metre of Internet

Kherson will forever remain Russian. Banners with this text stared back at the people of Kherson for nearly eight months. They were torn down as soon as the occupiers fled the city. You can still see remnants of these slogans, torn from their base, here and there. Soon, these will be covered up. "Forever" turned out to be quite short.

The occupiers stole and carried away all sorts of things, from agricultural equipment to the Internet. One Buryat warrior wanted to take the Internet with him. He allegedly cut himself a metre-long piece of internet cable from a house, saying he wanted to bring the Internet to his hometown.

Kherson is believed to have been founded by empress Catherine the Great's (Catherine II) favourite and lover, prince Grigory Potemkin. From 1781 to 1786, under Potemkin's guidance, the St. Catherine's Cathedral was built in Kherson, where Potemkin was later buried in 1791.

The tomb chamber, covered with a stone slab, can be accessed via a hatch in the church floor. That's precisely where grave robbers (most likely competent bone experts from the Russian Federal Security Service) climbed into the tomb chamber, ransacking Potemkin's remains and carrying them away. Vladimir Saldo, head of the Russian-occupied government of Kherson Oblast, reported the grave robbery on October 26. There were about two weeks left until the liberation of Kherson. So every occupier got something. Who got Potemkin's bones, who got a metre of internet cable. Who got cremated at the city dump.

There've been some interruptions in this cathedral's timeline. After the so-called October Revolution in 1917, the Bolshevik authorities turned it into a museum of atheism. During the German occupation, the church's activities were restored. In 1962, during a campaign against religion, the church was turned into a warehouse. It was used for storing lumber. In independent Ukraine, it became a church once again.

Father Andriy shows me Potemkin's tomb chamber. He's the church deacon. We don't crawl into the chamber; there's nothing interesting there. What's interesting is Father Andriy himself and that's what today's story is about.

Father Andriy is 44-years-old. He is a Ukrainian patriot who serves in the church — the Catherine II Cathedral, the legal status of which is unclear to me. Father Andriy insists that it is a Ukrainian Orthodox Church. I go there with the knowledge that it is a church under the Moscow Patriarchate. During this extensive war in Ukraine, church life has also undergone many changes. Father Andriy confirms that many churches previously under the Moscow Patriarchate have, during the war, distanced themselves and effectively become Ukrainian Orthodox churches. A natural and logical development.

In early March, FSB (Federal Security Service, Russia's successor to the NKVD and KGB) officers came to the cathedral and took Father Andriy away. A bag was pulled over his head in the car. Taken who knows where — the exact location isn't known by father Andriy himself. In any case, it was a well-equipped torture chamber. Interrogation. "Who do you know from the SBU (Ukraine's Security Service)?" they asked. "We have information that you collaborated with them. You went to Moscow in 2009." Indeed, Father Andriy went to Moscow in 2009 to perform with his fellow parishioners during Christmas. They sang Christmas carols. In Ukrainian, this singing tradition is called *колядования* ("koliaduvannia"). And in March of 2022, Father Andriy is accused of collaborating with the SBU for singing in Moscow thirteen years prior. It could not be that he went there just to sing. Agents open their computer, and Father Andriy sees his Facebook page there containing posts supporting Ukraine and memes ridiculing Russia.

Father Andriy is beaten. These men know how to beat someone. Nerve points on the legs. Hits to the head but not directly with fists. A thick book is placed in between to prevent visible bruises. It doesn't diminish the pain, though. Electrodes are attached to his index fingers. Electric shock torture begins. Andriy is forced to drink a sour-tasting alcoholic mixture that has an effect lasting several days. His hands and feet are tied up.

The torturers push the bound Andriy face down onto the floor and begin tearing his pants off. This is the breaking point. Father Andriy signs a phony document giving his resignation from his clerical duties. His hand is shaking from the electrical torture, making it difficult to give a proper signature.

Five hours have passed since the start of the interrogation and torture. Andriy is released. It's past curfew. "I can't go," he says. "They'll take me again." He is driven home by car. Full service.

Father Andriy stays at home for three weeks and then starts going to the church again. Initially, to sing in the choir and then he started conducting Sunday services again. FSB officers were always present, but they didn't take him away again.

The Ukrainian flag flew in Andriy's garden until the end of July. It wasn't visible from the street. Then came certain responsibility-baring comrades and took the flag away. Father Andriy thinks someone reported him.

Father Andriy tells me a story about Father Igor. At the beginning of the occupation, Igor managed to save seventeen Ukrainian soldiers from the Russians on the left bank of the Dnipro River. He gave them civilian clothes, hid their weapons and equipment in the church basement. The FSB arrested him. He's still imprisoned on the left bank, in Chaplynka.

How many collaborators were among the clergy in Kherson? Father Andriy estimates ten to fifteen. They all left with the occupiers. He highlights one name: Gennady Shkil. This man exposed many fellow clergymen who supported Ukrainian independence. He left for Russia with his two cleric sons.

When the Ukrainian army arrived in the city, many residents couldn't believe it at first. They thought it was a provocation, that these were Russian soldiers dressed up as Ukrainians. Father Andriy was initially cautious as well. How to discern whether they're really ours? Language. Pronunciation. In Ukrainian, there's one word that non-Ukrainians can never pronounce perfectly. That word is *паляниця* ("palianytsia"). Palianytsia is a simple home-baked Ukrainian bread. Russian soldiers and saboteurs who dressed as and called themselves Ukrainians, were caught by their mispronunciation of this word. They couldn't correctly palatalise the consonant cluster ц ("ts"). Last spring, near Bucha, I tried. I didn't pass the test. But I didn't pose as a Ukrainian nor am I some kind of saboteur.

When the FSB sadists started torturing Father Andriy, they asked him about his ethnicity. Ethnicity is not indicated in the Ukrainian passport. Father Andriy said he didn't know. One grandfather was Russian. The other one was Polish. One grandmother had Jewish roots. And finally, the other grandmother — his mother's mother — was Estonian from Southern Estonia. Father Andriy's mother was born in Pechory.

Father Andriy is, of course, Ukrainian. A Ukrainian with Estonian roots.

Artem's Journey From Mariupol to Kherson

Artem wouldn't be in Kherson now if he hadn't punched a DNR Colonel over in his hometown of Novoazovsk back in January of this year. Novoazovsk is a Ukrainian city that remained under the administration of the Donetsk pseudo-Republic after the battles of 2014.

23-year-old Artem worked as a bartender. In the wee hours of one night, a man who later turned out to be a high-ranking military man started picking a fight with him. He hit Artem in the face. He then was on the receiving end of a proper punch. The colonel called in seven subordinates who beat Artem up badly. Then the beating was continued by police officers who arrived on the scene. The surveillance camera had conveniently stopped filming at a suitable time for them. The colonel's attack was "not found" in the footage.

Artem contacted his uncle who works as the captain of a fishing vessel in Mariupol and told him what happened. His uncle strongly urged him to come to Mariupol. Artem left his hometown on January 14, 2022.

Artem had been under the influence of the Russian-made brainwashing industry since the age of fourteen. How very much he had heard about what sadists and murderers the militants of the Azov battalion are. How Bandera's people and nationalists kill children. Artem admits he was afraid when he arrived in Ukraine. It had been instilled in him that Russian-speaking people from the DNR were hated there.

Artem started working as a cook on a fishing boat in Mariupol. It stood in a small private port in the immediate vicinity of the Azovstal factory. Artem never met any child-eaters.

The pre-war weeks in Mariupol. Artem goes to sea, earns a decent salary. Enjoys freedom and the beautiful city. This all comes to an abrupt end.

The methodical destruction of Mariupol has begun. Most of the ship's crew members have left—gone home. Artem's home is on the ship. He stays there with a couple of companions. There's a generator on the ship. There's water. There's food. The Russian army's fire is focused on Azovstal. The port is right next to it. A near-by ship gets hit. A mine falls in the bow of Artem's ship too. In a metal ship, this creates such a resonance that those inside experience a severe shock. A week after the war breaks out, the ship's survivors decide to make their way to the Mariupol Drama Theatre in the heart of the city. At that moment, they don't yet know that the heart of the city is gone. It has been destroyed.

In peacetime, getting from the port to the theatre took about 40 minutes. It takes Artem two days. He ends up alone during the journey. His companions take shelter with acquaintances. The word shelter sounds out of place here, though. They're hiding in basements onto which the apartment building could collapse at any moment.

Artem stays in various basements. In one of these basement shelters, a young woman has gone into labour. People help out any way they can. Artem helps. The baby is born beautiful, alive and healthy. Artem goes outside to smoke. His hands are shaking. He sees a fire nearby, with some kettles on it. He goes to the campfire. At that very moment, a bomb falls on the house. Everyone in the basement dies. The life of the newborn child lasted about fifteen minutes.

Artem reaches the theatre. About two thousand people have gathered there. A building with thick walls seems to offer some semblance of safety in this hell that the city has become. People are hoping that an evacuation will be organised from there. Artem checks himself in. He finds a place to sleep on the third floor. The music school across from the theatre is hit by a missile. The theatre's windows shatter. Broken glass falls on Artem, who was sleeping under a window. He didn't suffer any serious wounds. He goes downstairs to the concert hall. Artem had once performed there as a kid. In the morning, he feels as though he has to leave. Two hours later there was no theatre anymore.

Artem walks for four full days to reach Berdyansk. Guard posts. "Why aren't you serving in the DNR Army?" There's a tattoo on Artem's leg. An angel and what not. He explains to the Kadyrovian that the image depicts the victory of good over evil. He got it to please his religious grandmother. "I believe in Allah," the Kadyrovian mumbles. Artem is able to pass.

It's a long way to Kherson. The last guard post before the occupied city. Artem has to undress. There's a bruise on his right shoulder. When he went and took down the Ukrainian flag on his ship in Mariupol and started taking it back to the cabin, the ship was rocked from an explosion. Artem hit his shoulder on an iron staircase, the shoulder got hurt. The inspectors are convinced that the bruise is the result of a gun—like when an automatic kicks back against the shoulder. Artem is able to convince them otherwise.

Kherson. He's out of money. For his last hryvnias, Artem buys a pack of cigarettes. In the shop, he sees a friend from his hometown of Novoazovsk. The friend comes through for him. Artem arrives at a refugee reception centre thanks to his advice and help.

It's a building in which a hotel used to operate before the war. Рішельєвський is the name of this hotel in the Ukrainian language. It's only after much puzzling that I realise the hotel is named after Cardinal Richelieu.

At the beginning of the war, even before the occupation, the hotel management decided to open a refugee centre there. On March 1, 2022, the first residents arrived—from the Antonovka district of Kherson. Their homes had already been destroyed by then.

Evheny, the hotel's director, kept the refugee centre running with his staff for the entire duration of the occupation. People were well housed and fed. And there have been thousands of them living in the centre, some staying for longer, others for a shorter time. Even now, people who have lost their homes live there, mostly women and children. It has been a large-scale humanitarian project, the nature of which the occupiers could not comprehend. "Why are you doing this? What do you get out of it?"

From June 20 on, Artem also lived at the centre. Artem is a trained chef. So now he's worked there as a chef to this day. It is actually at the centre's restaurant that I meet him.

Are you a good cook? Everyone praises my cooking, Artem says with a grin. It's like I've found a family here. We are all like a big family. I'm already a godfather to three children who have lived or are living here.

The last child that Artem became godfather to is Karolina. Karolina's going to be two soon.

Family. Artem's mother died when he was eight. Dad then brought a new woman into the house. An alcoholic. Artem grew up with his grandmother, the same one who is deeply religious. Grandma has since arrived in Crimea. She believes not only in God, but also in Putin. In her icon corner, there's an icon of St. Nicholas (*Nikolai Chudodvorets*) and a photo of Putin side by side. On July 2, Artem called his grandmother in Crimea to congratulate her on her birthday. Grandma turned 81.

Grandma — the one who raised him from the age of eight — did not accept Artem's congratulations. "You're a Bandera supporter and a fascist," she said. That was their last contact.

I love making Ukrainian borscht, Artem says. I myself have a sweet tooth. When I put cookies in the oven, the smell brings all the kids running. They wait to get cookies.

We're about to leave the centre just as the air raid sirens go off. We're advised to wait. I see Artem heading to the shelter with a little girl in his arms. The goddaughter Karolina? Karolina.

We learn that an 8-year-old boy was killed in that same missile attack on Kherson.

The Black Box Under Bakhmut

December 6, 2022, in the village of Ivanovsky near Bakhmut. A building where there is a Ukrainian army unit being stationed gets struck by a Russian Uragan rocket. The Uragan rocket is a cluster munition—upon reaching its target, the munitions in its container explode. Many of those inside the building lost their lives. I don't have the exact numbers, but Konstantin, who is telling me this, mentions figures between twenty and thirty.

Among the fighters who perished in that building were those individuals who found and brought with them the black box—a flight data recorder of a Russian SU-25 fighter jet that was shot down. It is unknown what their intentions were. To keep it as a souvenir? To sell it? A black box is used in an aircraft to determine the circumstances that caused the plane to crash. The box emits radio signals to help locate it. This box did too. Based on those signals, the Russians fired the Uragan rocket at the house.

Once the rocket had done its destruction, soldiers from the neighbouring building rushed out to help and rescue those who still could be saved. After they exit, another rocket lands on that building. Nobody is killed. The house was left empty just moments ago. Would the rockets have landed without the signal from the black box? Who knows?

The soldiers find the remains of a downed Russian SU-25 fighter pilot. More accurately, they found the charred remains of his body. At some point, these remains will be exchanged for living captured Ukrainian soldiers. The body of the dead pilot and the black box of the plane take lives, save lives, and grant freedom.

A Ukrainian fighter, going by the pseudonym Tundra, brings the shell of the death-dealing Uragan rocket to a camping equipment store in Kyiv. Near the store's entrance there is a small room that the storekeepers proudly call a museum. On the rocket's shell Tundra has written: *We fight for our home, our children, and for our free will.* Tundra is an alpinist and hiker. A year ago, he planned to conquer one of Nepal's 8000 metre peaks. Then the war began. Nepal and the mountain will have to wait.

In the war museum of the camping store, there are many painful exhibits. A notebook of a deceased Russian soldier with a photo of a beast on the cover and a beauty on the opening page. There are names and phone numbers of his parents and friends. On the first page there are phone numbers belonging to girls named Lena and Elena, to his friend Nikita and below them his mother's number. The mother knows where her son died and where his body is. If possible and the information is available, Ukrainian officials inform the relatives of fallen Russian soldiers about the death of their son. I could call this soldier's mother. I have her number. Maybe I'll call one day. I couldn't right now.

Thanks to the storekeepers, I get to speak with a fighter from the Azov Battalion who survived imprisonment in Russia. Vladimir is twenty-six years old. He was born and studied in Western Ukraine, in Lutsk. He worked in Poland for two years before the war. When the war began, he immediately returned to Ukraine to defend his homeland. He fought in Bucha. Joined the Azov Battalion. He arrived in Mariupol in early March of 2022. Like most battle-hardened soldiers, he doesn't talk much about himself. The hardest part is seeing people die, he says.

Mariupol. Close combat with Russian units on the right riverbank. At a distance of 200-300 metres. Retreat to the Azovstal factory complex begins in April. The distance with the enemy is at times reduced to nothing, even fighting within the same building.

The day arrives when the order to surrender is given. On May 18, fighters leave their shelters. It's the beginning of captivity. Initially, the prisoners are taken to the settlement of Olenivka, near Donetsk. This is the same place where on July 29, occupiers orchestrated an explosion that killed 53 Ukrainian prisoners and injured 75. Vladimir doesn't witness this. Just seven days after being arrested, he and hundreds of fellow prisoners are taken on Kamaz trucks to the Taganrog pre-trial detention centre. Data collection—photos, fingerprints, hair—for DNA analysis.

Interrogations. Two people per cell. A walk outside to get air is permitted once a week, for five minutes. The summer passes in captivity. "I can't talk about it in much detail right now," says Vladimir. "A lot of soldiers are still in captivity—the information I share could potentially worsen their situation."

The hope for release through exchange of prisoners. The information that some prisoners have already been exchanged doesn't reach Vladimir. Hope is abstract. One hundred and twenty days of captivity. Two hundred and fifteen prisoners are taken to an airfield. Among them are ten foreigners and five leaders of the Azov Battalion. They're flown to Belarus. Vladimir has a feeling that this must be liberation.

The Belarus-Ukraine border. Prisoners on the other side are waiting for release as well. On the evening of September 21, at around seven, Ukrainian fighters arrive home. They are taken to Chernihiv. Medical examinations. Starved bodies demand food, especially sweets. Many overindulge at first. Too much chocolate and candy at once.

A few days later, Vladimir arrives in Poltava and is reunited with his mother, sister and girlfriend. Vladimir falls silent for a moment. It's the only moment during our interview when he allows his emotions to surface.

Vladimir's weight upon release is 40 kg. Before the war, he was into bodybuilding. Even when fighting in Mariupol he weighed 120 kg. He lost two-thirds of his body weight during captivity.

Vladimir tells me that on January 16, 2023, during a rocket attack in Dnipro, his fellow prisoner and comrade from the days of fighting in Mariupol was killed—a woman. The woman's husband is still imprisoned and most likely doesn't know yet that she has died. Will you go back to combat? "Yes," Vladimir answers. "Most likely. I haven't signed any documents that would prohibit me from doing so."

Volodomyr's Three Battles Under Bakhmut

We meet with Volodomyr in the city of Pokrovsky. On its second day he joined the war. Volodomyr reached Bakhmut on February 25 as a member of the territorial defence unit. Territorial defence units are designated to specific areas. This means that if the ZSUs (Ukrainian Defence Forces) units there are moved elsewhere, the territorial defenders will remain in place — on their territory. They will be joined by a new incoming unit.

In July, the war under Bakhmut grew very fierce. At the end of July, Volodomyr, hiding in a trench, counts the explosions of shells fired by the Russians. The shells fall on the territorial defense's positions every 90 seconds on average. And so every day, for many hours. The length of the protected line is five hundred metres. A thousand or so shells fall on this line. There are twenty-eight defenders. For every defender, the Russians shoot out about thirty-six shells a day. Coupled, of course, with other weapons — Grad rockets, mortars, aircrafts.

Territorial defence fighters have built proper pillboxes on the line of defence. By the end of July, there are three left. There is no forest growing by the defensive line any longer. It has been mowed down by projectiles. Seventeen cars are destroyed. The defenders are alive. They're divided amongst the three pillboxes. On July 31, at seven o'clock in the evening, the Russians begin an infantry attack. The attackers are Wagner mercenaries. This comes out later.

For the majority of the men in the territorial defense, this is their first major battle. Among them are three or four men with previous war experience. The advice of the latter is to never shoot at attackers on a whim, in order to keep their exact location a secret for as long as possible.

For Volodomyr, a man of fifty, this is his first big battle. Affect and hysteria — the words he uses to describe the feelings during the first few minutes. Aimless firing from an automatic weapon. Only after changing the magazine is a sense of rational thinking restored. The opponent is 40-50 metres away.

The unit receives an order to retreat. The first dead. The ZSU's unit kicks the Wagner troops back the next day. Territorial defenders have killed over twenty Wagner soldiers the previous day. It was a unit of professionals. Sending prisoners to the *killing machine* has yet to begin.

Ten days later, the unit comes under another attack. This is the second big battle for Volodomyr. The defenders have dug themselves some trenches. They're shallow, you can only lie in them. A shower of shells, once again. Some men in the trenches die. Volodomyr lies in a trench close to his friend Vitali. The trench is built zigzag. They can only see each other's feet as they lie there.

A projectile falls into the trench. Volodomyr flies against the trench wall. Loses consciousness. When he regains consciousness, he sees legs protruding from around the corner. Those are Vitali's legs. In the same place as before. Volodomyr calls out to Vitali, talks to him. About ten minutes go by. Then he sees that he was talking to the legs, not the man. Vitali's body is no longer attached to his legs.

Volodomyr's third battle. After the concussion, he is moved twelve kilometres from the front line. He's now a barrack warden. A rocket falls on the building. Half of the building collapses. Volodomyr is pinned under the rubble. Fate has created a precise space between two panels for him. Or was it God.

Chaplain Dionissi's Service

Chaplain Dionissi is a somewhat burly 35-year-old man with a thick beard. I meet him in Sloviansk at his place of service. The chaplain's room is filled with religious icons. An altar stands by the window. There's something resembling a studio setup in the corner. A proper microphone on a stand and a computer. From here, Dionissi does live broadcasts to a Christian radio station once a week.

Yevgeni worked as a priest's assistant until he was sixteen. His father was a champion athlete in boxing. An atheist. Partial to alcohol. Yevgeni's life choices didn't meet his father's expectations. His father disowned him. He stopped calling him his son, disdainfully referring to him as *bogomolnyi* ("pious") instead. Yevgeni's father passed away when he was sixteen.

We'll skip over a significant portion of Yevgeni's life which included studies at a vocational school and work as a chef. His studies at Orthodox seminaries in Kharkiv, Zhytomyr, and Kyiv. Seven years of serving as the head of a monastery. Then the events of Maidan happened. By that time, he had moved to Eastern Ukraine and become a priest of a small-town church. Yevgeni was now known as Dionissi. He attended the Maidan protests in November of 2013, showing his support. He embraced the infectious spirit of the movement. Several members of his congregation were also involved in the Maidan events.

By the year 2014, Dionissi had moved to Sloviansk. In mid-April of 2014, Russian units occupied the city with the support of Donetsk separatists. Three knocks on Dionissi's door. He goes to open it wearing a pair of shorts and a T-shirt. Three men with assault rifles are waiting at the door. "You're coming with us. You'll never need to change clothes again."

Dionissi is taken to a Tsarist era prison in Druzhkivka. To a cell in its basement. He is interrogated every two hours, day and night. The prison is filled with detainees. Some of them are brought to the prison yard and shot. Dionissi can see this from his cell window.

Those set to be executed are brought in front of the garages that enclose the yard. They are shot with assault rifles. Those firing are not in Dionissi's field of vision. Not everyone dies immediately. Some are wounded. A vehicle backs up to the garage, both the dead and wounded are thrown in the back. The dead aren't the ones screaming. The vehicle drives away. What happened to the wounded? Presumably, the unfinished job was completed somewhere in the woods, where the murdered were also buried. Over the course of three nights, Dionissi had witnessed the killing of approximately thirty people.

On the third night, a masked man enters Dionissi's cell. "We are going to let you go. Sign this paper stating that you agree to leave the city within twenty-four hours — or your body will be floating in the river."

Dionissi signs the paper. He starts to leave. A terrible fear accompanies him — the fear of being shot in the back. "We all want to live after all," says Dionissi.

Where to go? His friends take him to a village near the city for refuge. He hides in a house for two weeks. On July 6, news arrives that Ukrainian forces have liberated the city.

Fast forward to 2017. Dionissi becomes the chaplain for a military unit based in Sloviansk. This is the same place where I met him. What did the war bring into his life and work? What's the most challenging part of this job?

The most challenging part is when men come and confess to him that their wives, whom they've sent away from the war to Europe, have abandoned them. They've found new love and are starting a new life in a new land. Does that happen a lot? Yes. I don't know what to tell them. These men who've sent their wives and children away, are here right now for the sole purpose of protecting those very same women and children. This is what the chaplain shares with me.

Fighters die every day. Dionissi sends them off each week. Trying to find words that will console their loved ones. Those are difficult to find. The most recent funeral? Day before last, on Saturday, in Barvinkove. A twenty-seven-year-old boy. He died near

Kreminna. He had only just joined the armed forces in January. Coffins are often not opened at funerals. That wasn't the case this time. The young man in the coffin looked as if he was asleep. His mother clings to his legs. His sister puts her arms around him. "All of this stays with me afterwards," says Dionissi. "I head back to my room. Can't sleep. Images of the funerals run through my mind. The people mourning. I call some colleagues. I talk. I cry. I need to release this pain. Otherwise I'll break on the inside."

This military unit has also been hit by Russian rockets. It is a TARGET. It's in the crosshairs. When will the next ones land, no one knows.

About a week ago some men were killed who were retrieving bodies from the front lines. The codename for the mission was *Cargo 200*. This time, they were retrieving the bodies of dead Russian soldiers found in the already liberated areas. They backed up onto a mine. One of the casualties was a twenty-year-old, named Denis Sosnenko. Dionissi doesn't know what happened to the bodies of the Russian soldiers. Perhaps their remains were loaded onto another car?

Denis was killed by a landmine, buried by Russian soldiers, while he was retrieving the bodies of fallen Russian soldiers. So that they could be identified through DNA testing and one day be sent to their families for burial. Dionissi tells me all this at the cemetery, right by Denis' fresh grave.

Notes on Dead Villages

Bohorodychne is a village next to the town of Sviatohirsk, on the other side of the Siverskyi Donets river. The name Bohorodychne contains two meaningful words — God and childbirth. Is this village born of God? It probably is, just like everything in this world. Right now it doesn't look like God is home. Bohorodychne is a dead village. There isn't a single house intact, nor do we see anyone there.

There is one living thing there, though. A starved dog sits on the road, probably in front of his house. Guarding and waiting. Hoping for the owner's return. Alexander, with whom we travel, takes a can of meat from the car and opens it. The can is frozen. He tries to pick the meat out with a knife, but the hungry dog manages to eat it all even without the help. The dog is missing a paw on one of its front legs — has it been ripped off by mine shrapnel?

Another animal catches our eye. A big white teddy bear is lying on top of a car wreck. Who used to play with it? Why has it been brought outside? Did a fleeing Russian soldier want to take it home to his little brother? I guess it didn't fit in his tank or car. It was still lying there when we left.

The first people we catch a glimpse of are in the nearby village of Dolina. No one lives in this destroyed village anymore either. Jelena and Yevgeny have come to the ruins of their home and are trying to repair the war-ravaged tractor. It's a big K-700. The first tractor that Evgeny owned, bought just before the war. Named it Brodjaga — The Vagrant.

Before getting his own machine, Yevgeny worked using borrowed tractors for several decades, saving up enough money to buy his OWN tractor. Two tractor tires, blown by bullets, have been replaced with new ones. Spring is just around the corner, soon Yevgeny will want to take to his field with his tractor. I don't know where Jelena and Yevgeny get all this strength from. "Fine, my home's been practically leveled, but its still my own." All that's left of their home is a pile of junk. They set free fifteen pigs out of their barns just before fleeing from incoming bombs and shells. Who knows what the pigs did with their new-found freedom. "None of them have returned. We saved up every penny to make our home better and more beautiful," says Jelena.

Yevgeny was born fifty-four years ago as one of a set of triplet brothers. One brother is dead. The other went off to St. Petersburg a few years ago to work as a coffin maker. He, no doubt, has his hands full there. And the third is trying to breathe life into his Brodjaga.

When Jelena and Yevgeny fled the village, their dog, named Boy, was on the run — perhaps fear of explosions drove him to run away. The dog's name was written on his collar. When they returned half a year later, phone numbers had been left on the inside of their refrigerator door, offering information regarding the whereabouts of Boy. The dog had probably come home to look for the family, and volunteers must have found him there and taken him with them. There is still hope that Boy is alive and well and will one day return home.

We reach the next village. There we meet three women — three widows. A mother, her daughter and sister. I won't name the women nor the village, because they asked for even their first names not to be written down. There is fear, not unfounded unfortunately, that the Russians might occupy the village once more. The village head draws up lists of evacuees. Women keep up to date with the movement of the front lines. They know exactly which roads taken away would mean they couldn't flee from the village. One of the sisters remained in the village for the entire duration of the occupation and does not intend to leave her home under any circumstances.

It takes time for fragments of the occupation to surface. How did the occupiers sustain themselves? They drank a lot — and it wasn't water. Before leaving they stole and took all sorts of stuff with them. For some reason, Buryats used the garage as a toilet. They had the habit of peeing in a bottle. Diversity enriches. In one house, Burjat soldiers were seen wearing women's dresses. Apart from that, they conducted themselves in a normal manner and didn't bully the villagers. Three Ukrainian territorial defense men were killed in the village. One of them hid in one of the houses — he perished along with it when the house was set on fire.

The widows talk of butterflies. These are plastic mines that explode when you step on them. The occupiers have scattered quite a few. There have been victims. These mines don't kill. They tear your leg off. The women know of three cases where people have stepped on a butterfly and lost their leg.

The widows share another strange story. A beautiful girl, Nastya, is said to have lived and might still live in Izyum. When she was told that God is beautiful, Nastya had replied, "I am more beautiful!"

The girl more beautiful than God then got into an accident soon after that, one which left her face disfigured. This all happened four years ago.

Deaths of Volunteers in Soledar

Andrew Bagshaw and Chris Parry lost their lives in Soledar on January 6, 2023. They had driven there to evacuate an elderly woman. They were actually on their way to Bakhmut when they received a request from volunteers working in Kramatorsk to pick up the elderly lady. Bakhmut had to wait. The men changed course and headed towards Soledar.

Andrew was a 47-year-old talented and renowned geneticist from New Zealand who had been living in England before coming to Ukraine. 28-year-old Chris was a running coach from England. He arrived in Ukraine on March 5, 2022.

In Kramatorsk I meet Olga. She's a volunteer who has, along with these men, saved hundreds and hundreds of people from the war. Olga met Andrew in July of the previous year. They didn't share a common language. Olga doesn't speak English. Andrew couldn't speak neither Russian nor Ukrainian. They communicated with the help of Google Translate. Upon speaking into your phone, the app generates a written translation that appears on your partner's screen.

Their first joint trip to Bakhmut to evacuate people from the war. Olga suspects that Andrew could be a Russian spy. He entered strange sequences of numbers and letters into his laptop. Olga believed it was coded text. Olga's big question: WHY did this man come to Ukraine? How is this his war? "I couldn't comprehend it. I couldn't understand what brought this person here," says Olga. "Would I go to a foreign country if there was a war there? No, probably not."

And how strangely and reservedly Andrew behaves. He doesn't express his emotions. When mines explode, Olga screams and drops to the ground, while Andrew barely nods his head.

For about a week, Olga suspects that Andrew could be a Russian spy. Then she found out that he is a geneticist. The marked sequences he manipulates with on his computer, are tools for his research.

I Google Andrew's research topics. I realise that I don't understand any of it. But I'll paste here a couple of sentences with keywords from Wikipedia. It indeed resembles coded text: *a sequence consisting of two nucleotides is called a dinucleotide microsatellite (e.g., ACACACACA). A repeated sequence consisting of three nucleotides is called a trinucleotide repeat sequence (e.g., AGCAGCAGCAGC).*

Andrew treated people with the utmost respect. "He even showed respect for alcoholics," marvels Olga. "And he stayed by the bedside of a sick elderly person, holding their hand until the medics arrived. In Bakhmut, he revisited the children he had previously helped. He loved them deeply."

Andrew seemed lonely. Aleksander, my reliable fixer, suggested to Olga in the autumn that she integrate foreign volunteers into one team so that they could communicate with one another. Andrew was joined by Chris, a volunteer running coach.

Olga noticed that Andrew wasn't eating properly. He often had nothing in his fridge. Olga started bringing food to Andrew. Brought it to him herself, sometimes asking her husband to deliver it. Her husband had to tell Andrew that Olga would be offended if he didn't accept the food. Andrew accepted it.

Evenings were the time to make plans for the next day. Comprehensive work with information—discerning where it was safe to travel in a city under bombardment and where the risk was too high. This information was constantly updated.

On December 24 of the previous year, Olga had to leave Kramatorsk. Her mother, who lived in Poltava, had suddenly fallen seriously ill. Olga drove to the hospital where her mother had been taken. Olga saw Andrew for the last time on December 24. After some time had passed, Olga's husband, who was serving in the military, was wounded.

"We taught Andrew how to hug," says Olga. "We hug a lot here. He got used to us hugging him, but he never initiated it. But when I told him that my mother was seriously ill, he hugged me first!"

On January 6, contact was lost with Andrew and Chris. Communication lost, hope persisted. Maybe the men were still alive. Taken captive? Wagner mercenaries were fighting under Bakhmut.

They had a fixed price list that motivated them to keep captured foreigners alive. They were paid $7,000 for every living foreigner. For a dead foreigner with identification, the payout was $500. For unidentified foreigners without documents, they received nothing.

Andrew continued to carry out evacuation trips to Bakhmut. Even to areas where it was strictly forbidden to go. Areas on the other side of the river, where the risk of death had grown extremely high.

The Russians offered the Ukrainian side a *silent night* for Orthodox Christmas, from January 6 - 7. Olga hoped it would work. That it would make Andrew's trips safer.

On January 5, Olga scolded Andrew on Viber. Andrew had once again evacuated people from that area.

Here are excerpts from Olga and Andrew's last correspondence:

O: It's a trap! You can't go! Foreign troops are already there.

O: I'm sorry, Andrew. It's a deception. There aren't any people living there. That address is far beyond the river.

A: There are still many people living on the east side of the river. I've been there many times in the past two weeks. I will find the exact location. It could be safe there. If it's further east, then infantry battles are taking place there. If so, it's not wise to go there.

O: I already saw where it is! There aren't any living civilians there. The army's there. It's a bad address. I've already deleted it.

The conversation goes on for a long time. Olga tries to convince Andrew to give up reckless risks. The conversation also addresses cases where people who have asked for help often refused to leave their homes (read: basements). There were and are many such cases.

And we've made it back to January 6, when communication with Andrew and Chris is lost. Andrew and Chris, who are already on their way to Bakhmut, receive information from Kyiv. There a volunteer named Philip remotely manages information about people in need and tries to send rescuers to them. It's a kind of dispatcher's work in its own right. Philip asks Andrew and Chris to go to Soledar to evacuate an elderly lady. Communication with the men is lost.

On January 8, Olga calls Andrew's phone. It's rings. Nobody answers. Olga speculates that it's already in the hands of the Wagner Group.

Volunteers and the police begin to investigate to determine the fate of the men. A few days later, information is received from the Wagner militants that the men's bodies have been found.

The bodies are handed over to the Ukrainian side. They are presumably exchanged for dead Russian soldiers. The Russians have taken care of the foreign volunteers' bodies. They've been washed clean of blood, placed in black bags and in proper coffins, covered with red cloth.

On January 20, Andrew and Chris' bodies arrive at the morgue in Kyiv. Olga still has hope. Hoping that there's been a mistake and that the bodies handed over aren't Andrew and Chris'. Daniel, a volunteer from Kyiv who took the bodies to the morgue, gets a chance to identify them. He calls Olga. Yes, they are indeed Andrew and Chris.

Lyman. The People Near War

Lyman is a woeful place. A broken city with broken people. The war is near. The people we meet are afraid of a repeat occupation. Some of them await it. The Russians occupied this city at the end of May, 2022. They were driven out by October 1. The Russians are not far away. Apparently, they've inched closer to the city in recent days. Rockets fall on Lyman every day. The war is near. Actually, it *is* here.

Viktor

We stop the car. An old man treads slowly, dragging a grocery cart behind him. Viktor is going to the store to buy cigarettes. He's happy to talk to us.

Russian soldiers beat Viktor because he was singing in his home garden in memory of his mother. It was the anniversary of her death, July 22, 2022. Two men with automatic weapons came into the yard. Your Ukraine is no more, and will never be. "You can thank the gray hairs on your head that we beat you as little as we did," they said before leaving.

The song Viktor sang in memory of his mother included these lines:

> Ukraine, my Ukraine,
> after journeys long
> your son's faithful heart
> I'll leave at your threshold.

Victor's house has been bombed to pieces. He and his wife Svetlana live in the summer kitchen. Svetlana is a Russian who hates Putin, Viktor says.

Viktor's children from his first marriage live in the Saratov Oblast in Russia. If we had not attacked Ukraine, Ukraine would have attacked Russia five days later. Those were a daughter's words to her father living amid Russian bombings.

Lyuda

Lyuda stands at the gate of her house keeping an eye on the children. Her daughter Liza is nine. Ukrainian soldiers brought the children a toy car with pedals the day before. Well, it's actually meant for smaller kids, but it brings joy nonetheless. The neighbor's son Sasha has come to play too.

Lyuda has worked on the railroad all her life. There she's been a painter, a janitor and a guard. She and her daughter survived the bombings in the basement. In the basement, Lyuda memorised the Lord's Prayer. And here's another prayer she read there every night:

> When I lay me down to sleep,
> Mother of God is here with me.
> Angels by my side,
> Jesus Christ by my head.
> That which to the Lord, may I too be given.
> Amen.

From Ljuda, we find out that the children in Lyman go to school. This is not common in Ukraine right now. We locate the school.

Olga

Olga is a teacher at Lyman's school nr. 5. One of the classrooms in the cold and desolate school building is warm. It's heated with small cast-iron wood stoves. The class is filled with kids. All age groups together. Olga works with the younger ones face to face. The older students work with their teachers online.

Olga survived the occupation in Lyman, in her own home. Her eighty-eight-year-old mother wouldn't leave. So her daughter stayed with her.

I feel like everything's starting up again, says Olga. I'm already thinking of ways to heat the basement. The city does get bombed — rarely right now, though. We've gotten used to it. This means our sense of danger has also weakened. Which is very bad. I lost two colleagues during the occupation — Alla and Viktor. The missile fell right in Alla's room. Both she and her husband were killed. Viktor, a physical education teacher, was wounded. He died later. The students? Thank God they're all alive.

Natalya

Lyman is divided into two — the South and North parts. We're going to North Lyman. Alexander, my traveling companion and assistant, tells me that many of the people of North Lyman are pro-Russian. Be their homes destroyed, be their lodging in basements — it is very difficult to get rid of the chronic disease that is called the Russian worldview. A brief encounter with a young man who has come up from a basement for some fresh air. "I don't care who has this city," he says. "I'm not for or against anyone." What I want is to be left alone. There's something unpleasant about this guy, even the look in his eyes is kind of slimy. We move on.

Natalya

Natalya has come to the street to send off her daughter. She invites us in. Natalya lives on the ground floor of a five-storey building. Besides her, there is one other person living in this big building.

Natalya is seventy-one years old. This brave woman admits to living most of her life as more of a pro-Russian. The war brought great change to her world. "Ukraine did not attack Russia. Russia attacked Ukraine. We don't want their "Russian freedom" around here. We lived better off than the Russians do."

Natalya's father was Russian, her mother Ukrainian. Natalya has a brother. When they were growing up, the siblings agreed that Natalya would become a Ukrainian and the brother a Russian. So Mom and Dad wouldn't get offended. So they both could pass on their heritages. Is the brother who lives in Dnipro still a Russian? "My brother had a stroke. We can't ask him anymore," says Natalya.

A Cat Named Lyman

My aide Alexander takes me to see one of the basements and its inhabitants. "Anyone alive in here?" he shouts at the basement door. Not any more. Have the residents all left? Alas. A ginger cat starts circling us. He only has a short piece of his tail left. When we get in the car outside, the cat follows us to the car. Are you really leaving me here? This question is written all over his face. No, we're not. Alexander makes a call to Kramatorsk and comes to an agreement with Olga that we'll bring the cat to her. Later Olga will pass him on to animal welfare. This is the same Olga who told me about the deaths of Andrew and Chris.

Our day isn't over yet. With Alexander at the wheel, the cat in my lap, we drive to find Ruslan. Ruslan's taking us to the military unit, whose fighters are probably the cleanest on this front. They have a sauna built in Estonia at their disposal. The sauna and the fighters I met there will be covered in the next entry.

Estonian Sauna and Half of a Mother's Heart

This sauna is located... Well, it is where it is. In any case, on February 13, 2023, together with Aleksander, we embark on a journey to find this sauna somewhere in Donbas.

We drive towards Lyman. We work the entire morning and afternoon. Aleksander manages to get in contact with the military unit that has the sauna, crafted and also brought here by Estonians. They agreed to take us there. And they did.

It's a heartwarming feeling to see a fully functional sauna. Just heated. I step inside. Mauricio, a fighter from Colombia, is just finishing his sauna session and getting dressed. He doesn't speak English, nor do I speak Spanish. It's a shame. I can't even ask if it's his first time in a sauna. But he has a pleasant demeanor. I take a photo of him, as he's putting on his boots in front of the sauna.

I meet two British volunteer fighters next to the sauna. James and James. They're twenty-two and thirty years old. The older James is holding a machine gun. They're soldiers with experience, having fought near Kharkiv and liberated Izyum. The younger James hasn't started a family yet, but the older one has. He has a ten-year-old son waiting for him at home. He got a chance to go home for two weeks in September.

Just a couple dozen minutes ago, in a nearby village a Grad rocket had fallen near a house leaving an older man killed, and his wife injured. The younger James shows me a hole about ten metres from the sauna. Yesterday, a Russian drone dropped a bomb there. "Keep your eyes peeled and watch the sky," he says. Eyes peeled. We watch the sky.

Ruslan, who guided us to the military unit, takes me on a courtesy visit to the battalion's commander. The commander's words of gratitude to the Estonians for the sauna are sincere. I meet several other fighters. Amongst them is a bearded man sitting with a camera. French director Florent Marcie. He has been living and traveling with the battalion for four months. He has made films in plenty of war zones—Chechnya, Sudan, Libya, Afghanistan. I express my deep respect for him.

I'm back in my hotel in Druzhkivka. The place is filled with journalists from various countries. I haven't interacted with any of them during the ten or so days I've been here. In the evenings, I didn't have any energy left after a long day and in the mornings, I was too sleepy to exchange pleasantries in English. You can also come across Ukrainian fighters here, who are on a short break. In the evening, I happen to sit across from two fighters with whom a conversation sparks up. Alabai and Rezvii — these are pseudonyms. Alabai is another name for the Central Asian Shepherd Dog. Rezvii means 'sharp'.

Alabai was granted a four-day break. He still has a couple days of rest left. He's from a unit that no longer exists. He can't go back there after his break. He will join Rezvii's unit after his leave.

Alabai is from a Ukrainian-Belarusian border village in the Oblast of Chernihiv. He's forty-six years old. A father to a son, and a grandfather to a grandson. His mother suffered a heart attack seven years ago. Alabai says only one half of his mother's heart is functional. But the half that works worries about her son. She calls him frequently. The last time was this morning.

Pilots and Dead Bodies.
The Free and The Bound

Time to leave Donbas for now. Alexander takes me to Dnipro in his car. We have agreed on a meeting with three Russian prisoners of war. Three pilots. Allegedly the only pilots currently imprisoned in Ukraine.

We're going through Pavlograd, then continue on the open road. "Do you smell corpse?" Alexander asks me. Yeah, when I roll the car window down a little bit, some sort of stench permeates the car. Where's it coming from? Alexander points to a train with refrigerated carriages standing about seven hundred metres away on a side road. "Up to five hundred bodies of Russian soldiers have been stuffed into each wagon. The Russians are not interested in them, the bodies of their own remain on the battlefield. They are collected in refrigerated wagons. That's where they await their fate. These refrigerator cars are connected to power. The cooler is on, but they start decomposing rather quickly regardless."

We see several more rows of reefers like this on the way to Dnipro. If you can smell the stench of death from almost to a kilometre away, then how must it smell like next to the wagons? Thousands of decomposing bodies.

One of the reasons why Russia is not interested in taking them is, of course, economic. If a soldier stays missing, then they don't have to pay the family compensation, so-called *suffering money*, for the loss. Also, shoddily made cars—'Ladas' won't have to be given out to their widows and mothers. For the Russian authorities, it's as if the matter has been resolved. But not for Ukraine. There are no people, just their dead bodies. The question remains, how long can they be stored in this way.

We get to Dnipro, to the prison. I feel really sick. And I know why. What I experienced during imprisonment in Afghanistan nearly six years ago is resurfacing in me. I haven't been to a working prison since then.

Maxim

We wait in the visiting room. They bring in the first of three airmen. I'll make up first names and ages for all of them. Let him be Maxim and his age thirty-eight. Pilot of the bomber plane SU-34. A high ranking officer. In early March 2022, his plane was hit by a Ukrainian missile in the Kharkiv region. The pilot ejected. Tried to get to his own people. Was arrested.

What do we find out? That the bombs dropped on his flights over Ukraine did not hit the targets or kill any people. That he was following orders. That he only gets coordinates and drops the bombs according to them. He doesn't see where. He doesn't look down from the plane window. Why did Russia attack Ukraine? Don't know. It would have been better if they hadn't. Has any country attacked Russia in recent decades? After World War II? No. But they've tried to destroy us from within. They've tried to reshape our culture, our youth. When they make an exchange for your freedom, will you go back to combat? No. I'd retire. Ejecting exerts a huge strain on the body. It left serious consequences on my health. An X-ray was made of his back, doctors examined his condition.

In Russia, the pilot received a salary of 100,000 rubles per month. That's about 2,000 US dollars. Over there that's a lot of money. The food here? It's alright.

Ukraine has tried several times to exchange all three pilots for their own imprisoned soldiers. At the beginning of captivity, the pilots were taken to Chernigiv prison for a while. Hope faded when other prisoners waiting to be exchanged were taken away, but the pilots remained. Allegedly no 'price agreement' was reached. The second attempt was in Sumy. Once again, the Russians scratched the three pilots off the exchange list.

Could it be that this imprisonment has saved your life? If it wasn't for this, maybe you'd be dead by now? Sooner or later, you'll be free. "Yeah, that might be the case." Do you feel responsible for what is happening in Ukraine? "Yeah, it's really hard on me on a humane level."

With the help of the Red Cross, Maxim has been able to call his wife three times. Emails may be sent and received. How do you spend your days? We receive books. I read a lot. I'm Orthodox. I also have a Bible in my cell.

Maxim leaves. I shake his hand. He has a strong handshake. For a moment, he looks me very deeply in the eye. "When you are freed—don't fly over a second time," says Alexander. "I won't," he answers. Maxim then asks if we happen to have cigarettes. We don't have any. If we had known of the need, we would have brought some along.

Jura

Jura flew the bomber SU - 30 SM. He flew with a navigator. They dropped bombs on the old district of Kramatorsk. Their plane was hit by a missile. A BUK, Jura believes. He made a quick and sharp dive down to shake off the missile tailing him, but it didn't help. Both ejected. The wind took them to different places. When they landed, they couldn't find each other. Later, Jura learned that his companion had made it back to the Russian-controlled area.

Jura tries to get there too. First, he moves about thirty kilometres north. Arrives in Sviatohirsk. He hides in a cottage for a few days. There's a gas stove, with gas still in the cylinder, and some matches. He gets to boil water. To dry himself off a little. He finds a piece of lard and a jar of strawberry jam. A phone—a simple button phone is in his pocket. He calls his own. They promise to come pick him up at night. An exact location on a forest path is agreed upon. Jura waits there for one night. And another. He can still call. Yeah, we're coming. Wait. Jura waits. To no avail.

Ten days or so have passed. The phone's dead. Jura goes to the highway—a Russian airman in uniform—and stops a passing car. These are civilians. He asks if he can charge his phone. They let him. The car pulls off. In ten minutes, Ukrainian soldiers come to arrest Jura. Now we're at the part I never quite understood. Jura had a weapon. He had a grenade. "I would have resisted, but I couldn't," says Jura. "My hands were frozen." Three Ukrainian fighters encircle Jura. He surrenders. Everything was *culturno*, he says. I wasn't beaten. Alexander later thinks that Jura deliberately went to the highway and intercepted a private vehicle so that he would be reported. To surrender. To survive. He was lucky—the lives of occupiers are not always spared in such situations.

And now a few fragments of Jura's answers to our questions. Once I'm free, I won't fight anymore. I'm going to retire. I feel guilty about Ukraine. I have been rethinking my life here. I don't have a negative attitude towards Putin. Life in Russia has gotten better. I miss my family. I've never been abroad. Well, yes, now I have… I was shot down on my second flight to Ukraine, to North Kramatorsk. Our squadron was made up of eight aircrafts. The others turned back. The first flight I made was to Balakliia. I still feel that I am needed in my homeland.

During the ten days that Jura hid in the woods, his toes froze. His big toes were later amputated.

What do I do in the cell? I read books. At the moment I'm reading a book on archaeology by Andrei Nikitin. Back home? I played guitar, went skiing, played volleyball.

Jura's leaving. "Please don't fly here any more!" With those words, Alexander sends him away. "No, no I won't," the pilot answers.

Sergey

Sergey too wants his age to be put down as thirty-eight. He's from Karelia. His fighter jet was shot down in April 2022. He ejected, was immediately captured. He suffered a fracture while ejecting.

"I have a wife and kids at home. I haven't been abroad. I was following orders. I don't want to fight any more." Sergei is extremely tight-lipped. He's the only one of the three that I think is willing to continue on killing the people of Ukraine. I'm not sure how that'll end, though. Sooner or later, they'll be back home. Imprisonment may be the part of their fate that has kept them alive. Does that change their outlook on life and how so? I don't know, and I'm not likely to ever find out.

Cows and Butterflies in the Town of Kaminka

I watch a short video sent to me on my phone. In it, two cows are eating hay. The video's caption reads: Kvitka is on the left, her calf Liska on the right. They were killed by the first missile.

The video is followed by some photos — of a home still intact, a couple more cows, and some cats. One caption reads: *Julka – a cow who also fell victim to the first missile strike*. Another caption: *Out of four cats only one has survived, the one in the very back*.

Kaminka village in the Izyum district. Oleksandr and I originally had planned to go to Izyum. However, on our way there we see Ukrainian soldiers working on a destroyed Russian tank. We decide to stop and go talk to them. They are disassembling parts from the tank that can be used to repair their own tanks. Are there still people living in the village? No, there aren't. All the houses have been bombed to pieces. Be careful; the Russians have planted a lot of mines here.

We proceed with caution. The ground is covered with snow. When Oleksandr turns our car around, he moves it just half a metre at a time to avoid straying from the tire tracks. The side of the road mustn't be driven nor walked on.

We decide to follow tire tracks leading up to the village, in the hope of meeting someone. And we do. There's a man working near one of the houses. That's Volodomyr. He and his wife Ludmilla came back to see if there's anything to salvage in the ruins of their home. The walls of their summer kitchen are still standing. They've put up a tarp for a roof and they've got a fire going in the stove. There are at least seven cats eating cat food in the middle of the floor. Ludmilla makes coffee and slices a small kringle. We are guests in a warm shack, among people with warm hearts.

Before the war broke out, the village of Kaminka had around 800 inhabitants. Heavy battles in and around the village took place in March of 2022. On March 13, a tank battle took place. Ukrainian defences held up until March 26. The residents fled. The remaining few families were forcefully deported, loaded into Kamaz trucks by the Russians. Only a few remained behind. The Russians laid waste to the village, empty and reduced to rubble, until September 13. The Russians sure know how to ravage.

The Russians had to leave in a hurry. Massive amounts of ammunition, including hundreds of Grad rockets were left behind. From his own yard, Volodomyr gathered around 300 projectiles. These have all probably been "sent back" to the Russians by now. Ukrainians don't want what's foreign, but won't give up what's their own.

Volodomyr and Ludmilla are farmers, who have both graduated from the Kharkiv Agricultural Institute. Their home has been destroyed, their fields still remain. They've been coming back to the ruins of their home, from their temporary residence in Izyum, since September 23. They have four hectares of land just outside the village. Volodomyr checks on it every day — marking dangerous spots and clearing away debris. He's preparing for spring planting, but he doesn't yet know how he'll do it. All their machinery was destroyed.

They aren't the only ones who still visit the ruins of their homes. It's a small world. Volodomyr knows Sasha and Zhenya from the village of Dolyna, whom I wrote about earlier in this diary. A couple who were repairing a tractor near their destroyed home. Volodomyr knew of someone from their village, who recently stepped on a mine while working near their house. He lost a leg.

The Russians were in a big hurry to leave, but not in so much of a hurry as to not scatter some mines before they left. The main goal of these mines isn't to kill, but to maim. This little plastic mine has been given a couple of nice names. They are called butterflies or little leaves — they do indeed look like butterflies or small leaves. These butterflies take flight when even slight pressure is applied, around 5 kg. They will explode even under the foot of a small child. The fact that these mines only have a small amount of metal in them, makes the clearing of these mines a difficult task. When you step on them, the pressure causes the chemicals inside the butterfly's wings to mix, resulting in an explosion.

During the Soviet military intervention in Afghanistan from 1979 to 1989, about 1.5 million Afghans were killed in a campaign of mass murder. Has anyone counted how many people lost limbs due to these butterfly mines there? When I was travelling through Afghanistan from 2014 to 2017, I met such people everywhere. These mines continue to do their job many years after they are planted. They will continue to do the same in Ukraine.

Every excessive step taken in the village of Kaminka village carries a risk. Volodomyr once saw a butterfly mine staring back at him from between his two feet. It was partially hidden under sand. There's only one place in the village where you can feel safer — the frozen surface of the fish farming pond, there you can walk with confidence.

The water in the village wells is salty. People have been fetching drinking water from a nearby spring for generations. Its water is pure and tasty. The Russians didn't allow the few remaining villagers to access the spring. Volodomyr's friend Sergey was severely beaten after his attempt to collect water from the spring. We didn't meet Sergey, we later on did however visit his mother with Volodomyr and Ludmilla.

Volodomyr and Ludmilla stopped speaking Russian in 2014. They are however willing to speak Russian with me since I don't speak Ukrainian. Many people have made a clear choice regarding their language preference. Those who didn't make that decision in 2014, made it within the past year. We can never forgive what these people have done to us, says Ludmilla.

All the homeless cats from the village seem to have found shelter in Ludmilla and Volodomyr's summer kitchen. They talk about their cows that were killed — how much time and effort it takes to raise a calf that will eventually give milk, and how easy it is to kill it. They were able to bury one of their cows that was killed in the bombing. The skeleton of the other one is scattered around the outskirts of the village.

Volodomyr and Ludmilla radiate with hope and determination that they can rebuild their home, plow their fields, and acquire new cows. The ongoing war doesn't deter them. People need to eat during wartime as well.

They recount a story they heard from their grandparents about the famine that took place after World War II, in the years 1946-1947. When Russia continued its collectivization of Ukraine, destroying its agricultural community. This famine was smaller in terms of the number of victims compared to the Holodomor famine of 1932-1933. This fact, however, was no consolation to anyone who died of starvation in Ukraine at the time in question.

NKVD agents guarded the fields to prevent starving villagers from "stealing" grain. Starving children removed their clothes and crawled onto the fields to eat grain. Why take off their clothes? Because it was harder to spot the child's naked body amongst the yellow crops.

Oleksandr and I don't go to Izyum that day after all.

The Long Road to Becoming a Woman

This brave woman was born a boy. I don't know how she was baptised after she was born. I talk to Oksana on the phone for an hour. From her FB pictures, looks like a nice young woman.

Very many transgender people have contemplated, attempted or committed suicide. Oksana attempted suicide in 2012. Survived. Started preparing for a sex change. Underwent long-term hormone therapy. Oksana's gender reassignment surgery at the hospital in Zaporizhzhia was planned right for the beginning of the war. It was cancelled. Postponed. Oksana went to war on the second day of that war.

Oksana was born and raised in Donbas, in the city of Makiivka which conurbated with Donetsk. In 2014, she fled her hometown. She was targeted, picked up at her home soon after she left. A close relative, a cousin, complained to the new authorities about Oksana. A lumpen, an alcoholic, a separatist. This is how Oksana describes her cousin—a traitor who later died a traitor's death.

Oksana joined the defenders of Ukraine as a volunteer in 2014. Defending the Donetsk airfield. Do you remember the first person you killed? Oksana doesn't like the word "kill". "We "utilise" enemies," she says. "He was a *separyonok*, a little separatist. I took his automatic rifle. I fought for a month and a half with that weapon."

Early morning of February 24, 2022. Oksana hears explosions from her apartment in Kyiv. On the fourth day of the war, she is given a gun.

Oksana doesn't want to talk about combat. She talks about massive, chronic fatigue, emotional burnout. And knowing you can't leave. Behind you, in the rear, are your own.

Protecting Majorski. It's a town near Horlivka in Donbas. Russian forces encircle the settlement. The defenders manage to break the siege. Eighteen civilians in the settlement are murdered by the Russians. Oksana talks about an intercepted radio transmission where the Russians use the expression *grazhdanskih obnulitj*. That means eradicating civilians, murdering them. And eradicate they did.

The last few weeks have been very difficult. The army unit is fighting near Bakhmut. The company that Oksana began fighting under consisted of a hundred and twenty fighters. Only a third of them are in the lines now. Twelve fighters were killed last week, two more this week.

Oksana tells of a recent Russian landing operation in which the six of them fought a battle against a unit several times larger than their size. "We took 300s," she says. Meaning, the wounded were not left behind, they were taken along.

I call Oksana at the agreed upon time, she's busy. I'm training young boys, she says. Called back later. Who are they? Freshly mobilised, five boys. I taught them how to shoot from different positions. How do soldiers behave after the first battle? So many fall into a stupor. Then a couple of slaps and 200 grams of vodka will help. Not everyone can kill. Some people start running when they should instead be lying down. Ten thousand shots need to be fired before you can consider yourself an experienced soldier.

War directly exposes the substance of an individual, says Oksana. Shows you who's a real human being. In October, when we were defending Horlivka, we brought two wounded soldiers out of the line of fire. I met one of them when on vacation at the end of December. We hugged. We didn't talk about the rescue. There were six of us rescuers—we couldn't have done it alone.

On October 30 of last year, Oksana was wounded. A shrapnel wound to the leg. She was treated at Pavlohrad Hospital. She met an Estonian who was also being treated there—Toomas. Hemingway once said to have met at least one Estonian at every port (or port tavern?). There are probably more Estonians helping Ukraine now than we can imagine.

Have you taken anyone prisoner? No. We don't take prisoners. But you yourself—would you surrender? No. I always have a grenade with me. Let's call it a good-luck-grenade. I don't want to get tortured. That's what Oksana says.

She also says that she can tell from someone's eyes whether they've already been on the front lines. The gaze of these people, their glance is different. Death has looked them straight in the eye.

Alina, her partner, waits for Oksana at their Kyiv home. When the war is over, Oksana will start hormone therapy again. It can't be continued right now—too much of a strain on the body. After the war is over, the brave Oksana can finally reach the end of her long road to becoming a woman.

A Love Letter from a Russian Prison

Hello, my dears!
I am alive and well, no injuries. I have been in prison within Russian Federation territory for three months now.
   The attitude toward us is positive, the food is good, I don't go hungry here.
   Most importantly, don't forget my parents and try to keep them calm.
   I hope you are all well, that you are alive and healthy, and that the children are by your side.
   Tell the children that I'm counting on them to help you with everything.
   I love you all. Keep that in mind.
   I hope the leaderships of the countries will come to an agreement, and we will see each other again.
    Once again, I want to reassure you – I am alive and well. The most important thing is you – your health and wellbeing.
Don't forget – I love you all.

Sender: Sergei....
Recipient's address
2.06.2022
Seal: Verified on 02.06.2022

There is little truth in this letter. What is true is the sender's name, the date of the letter, and that the writer is in prison in the territory of the Russian Federation. What is true is that the writer cannot write the truth. What is true is that the sender loves his wife, children, and parents very much. This is a love letter.

   The letter's author is Sergei, a 45-year-old officer in the Ukrainian army's intelligence unit. These lines were written on the **four hundredth** day of his captivity. He spent most of that time in the city of Borisoglebsk's SIZO number 9, in Voronezh Oblast. What is SIZO? It's an abbreviation of the Russian phrase *Следственный изолятор*—a pre-trial detention centre. In reality, it's an overcrowded prison where people are tortured and starved.

On the morning of March 11, 2022, Sergei spoke on the phone to his wife Tamara for the last time. On that same day, Sergei and six of his fellow soldiers went on a reconnaissance mission to the region of Vuhledar, in the Donetsk Oblast. They were ambushed by Russians and captured. The ambushers were wearing Ukrainian army uniforms. On March 12, Tamara received an SMS from an unknown number. It contained the news that her husband had been captured. The text was sent from a phone that one of the detainees managed to hide at first. Thanks to this, many relatives learned of the imprisonment of their family members.

Sergei is a reserve officer, and his son Ivan follows in his father's footsteps. Ivan has been in active service as an officer since 2019. On February 23, Sergei joined his son in the Independent Intelligence Battalion in order to be as close to him as possible, if not physically, at least in the same region. So that both father and son can know and feel each other's presence nearby.

Sergei was sent to the front line on March 3. He went on multiple combat missions with his unit. I have already written about the events of March 11.

One SMS from March 12 and one letter that Tamara received two months after it was written. Tamara worked diligently to determine her husband's location. To gather information about the prison, Tamara went through the Telegram channels of Russian bloggers. SIZO number 9 is in Borisoglebsk. Tamara's 87-year-old grandmother Nastja lives in the same area. Nastja is Tamara's mother's mother. Tamara called her grandmother and other relatives. Could they go and visit Sergei? Bring him a care package? Fear has paralyzed these people. No, they can't do anything. Please don't call me again, says her grandmother. Tamara doesn't call her again.

Tamara hasn't told Sergei's parents that their son is in prison. She tells them that he's in a very special and secret position and isn't permitted to communicate much with the outside world. His parents believe her — or at least pretend to.

In April, two members of Sergei's unit were exchanged for Russian prisoners. Two out of six. On December 6, Colonel Oleg, who shared a cell with Sergei, was exchanged. On December 31, 20-

year-old Bohdan, who too was held in the same cell, was exchanged. Tamara met them both.

The attitude towards us is good, the food is good, I don't go hungry here, Sergei wrote in his only letter to Tamara. They were given food once a day — a bowl of porridge, Oleg and Bohdan told Tamara. There's video surveillance in the cell. During the day, they weren't allowed to sit or lie down — if they did, the guards would beat them. Medical help? 20-year-old Bohdan had been shot in the leg when he was captured. He wasn't treated, and the wound festered. Upon his release, doctors nevertheless managed to save his leg from amputation. How did Sergei hold up? He supported all of us, recounted stories from the books he had read and movies he had watched, said his cellmates. Yes, Sergei is very strong, says Tamara. I believe he'll endure.

The prisoners were taken outside for **half an hour once a month**. Does that add up to nearly **seven hours** out of the entire time he has spent in prison? *The attitude toward us is positive.*

On March 8 of this year, the Russian ombudsman published a list of prisoners that the Ukrainian government allegedly doesn't want to exchange for Russian prisoners. Of course, this is false, but it's a lie that very deeply hurts many people. It hurts Tamara too. The prisoners live in complete information isolation, she says. They know nothing about how well Ukraine has held up. They are lied to — they are told that Ukraine has essentially surrendered. Tamara saw a video leaked on social media a few days ago, showing Russian soldiers using a knife to behead Ukrainians. It filled her with terrible fear.

A couple of years ago, when the Taliban took control over Afghanistan, Sergei was on a peacekeeping mission in Kabul. The Taliban held him captive for a couple of weeks before he managed to return home. Could he have been in the same prison as I was in the spring of 2017? Maybe I'll get the chance to ask him someday. For now, all I can do is hope and pray that he survives and returns home.

Ascension Day In Donbas

It's early Easter Morning. Sunday. At least here in Donbas, people don't go to church that morning. Church services are brought outside. Gathering places, where the Passover service will be held, have been agreed upon. Churches full of people could otherwise become the target of Russian troops. The church in the village of Komishuvaha in the Zaporizhzhia district was hit by a missile on Saturday night. There were no people inside.

We go to the edge of the town of Druzhkivka with Alexander, my fixer. A table has been set up in front of a private home with the things necessary for the service. Father Dionissy, the military chaplain I met and wrote about in February, arrives.

I wrote then about Dionissy and of what happened in April 2014. The city was occupied. Occupiers took Dionissy to the basement of a prison in the city of Druzhkivka. Those arrested were shot in the prison yard. Dionissy saw it from his cell window in the basement.

Do you remember that story? Not everyone died right away. Both the dead and the wounded were thrown in the back of a truck. The wounded were screaming. What happened to the wounded? The unfinished work was then probably completed in the forest. Dionissy witnessed the murder of about thirty people over the course of three nights. For three nights, he waited for his turn to be put to death. Something like that stays with a person forever.

Back to the service, to the people. I get to talking with Leonid. The man, who was pushing seventy, went to the military commissioner on February 25, 2022, asking to be sent to the front lines. He became a mortarman in the territorial defense unit. It's a much safer job in war than being an infantryman, Leonid says. And tells the following story.

October 28, 2022 on the front line under Lyman. Leonid is in position with his mortar. Endless rain soaks everything. Including the sleeping bag he lays in. He finds a larger piece of plastic and wraps it around himself. If only the rain would stop, the freezing man pleads. Morning comes. The sunrise. A projectile falls near Leonid. No explosion follows. Another projectile falls. Silence. The night rain has made the earth so soft that projectiles fall into soft mud without exploding. The night rain saved Leonid's life.

Leonid isn't in combat anymore, but if needed, he'll go as a partisan. He talks about a poster put up by forest defenders in the forest near Lyman: "Protect the forest, otherwise there is nowhere to wage a partisan war!".

On April 14, 2023, Russian rockets fell on the residential area of Sloviansk. One of them hit a five-storey residential building. Press reports say that about eleven people were killed and several dozen wounded. We get to this house at around nine o'clock on the morning of April 16. Rescuers have begun their third day of rescue work. There are apartments and pockets underneath the rubble that they don't yet have access to. There might be more people in there. There is hope that they're alive. Hope is alive. I don't know about the people, though.

In the outermost stairwells of the building, life goes on. A man and a woman enter the first stairwell, a holiday pasha in hand. They're going to visit their daughter. I follow them. The daughter Tarja comes to the corridor and agrees to talk a little.

Tarja and her husband's friends lost their two-year-old son Maksim. They brought him out of the rubble, he died in the ambulance. Maksim's father, Sergey, has not been found. Three people have yet to be found, Sergei among them. Hope lives on. "Is it possible that Sergei was taken to the hospital and hasn't been identified," Tarja asks. People had seen a man who lost his limbs being taken away. Maybe it was Sergei?

Katyrina

Katyrina is a twenty-year-old military medic. She went into service immediately after the war broke out. April 14 was the most difficult day of her service to date. On April 14, she rescued fourteen-year-old Sofia from the rubble of a residential building hit by a missile in Slovyansk.

Katyrina wasn't called to the scene of the disaster. She just happened to be there with fellow members of the defence forces. The same explosion that killed those people, it's blast wave hit the car they were in, shattered the windows and hurled fragments through the car. Katyrina grabbed her first aid bag and joined the rescue efforts. Went up a dust-filled staircase to the fourth floor. Climbed over a pile of rubble, reaching the hole that rescuers said the child was in. She made her way to Sofia. One of the other rescuers stayed to help. Sofia's leg was wedged under a panel. She was conscious, but quiet. For four hours, Katyrina and the other rescuer worked side by side. The danger was that the wreckage could fall on them all. There was minimal room to help. Katyrina and the rescue worker had to share a helmet. When one was working by the child—since only one of them could fit at a time—the helmet was on their head. After the rescue worker had managed to create sufficient space, Katyrina was able to extend Sofia's hand over her head and hook her to an IV. Able to get her hooked to an IV. The rescue worker was keeping an eye on the panel above his head. They were on the fourth floor, onto which the fifth had fallen.

At one point, Katyrina was able to free Sofia's mangled leg and put a tourniquet on her thigh so that the poisonous substances formed in the injured leg would not spread throughout the body. Sofia was brought out, taken to the hospital. "Sofia didn't lose her leg," says Katyrina. She and her boyfriend want to visit her in a couple of days.

What else? When Katyrina had made her way to Sofia, lying under the rubble, she called Artur, her teacher from medical college. Artur is a surgeon who was wounded on the front lines in the fall. That's when Artur lost his leg. Now Katyrina received advice and encouragement from him on how to save Sofia's life.

"I didn't perceive time, didn't feel scared when I was with Sofia," says Katyrina. It was when I got home and was having tea that my hands started shaking.

Easter Sunday is coming to a close. Forty days from now, they will celebrate Christ's ascension to heaven. Maxim's already there. And who knows how many other innocent souls.

To Walk on Your Own Two Feet

Dima and Oksana. 21 and 25. They don't know each other, but through this story here, their paths cross. These are two young people whose legs were taken from them by the war.

Dima

I meet Dima in the village of Novofedorivka. He arrives at his house just as we do. Steps out of his car. Takes his crutches and sits on a bench at the side of the village street. The car is a regular one with an automatic transmission. Dima uses his prosthetic legs to push the pedals.

Dima became a soldier in 2020. At the beginning of the war, his unit was sent towards Izyum to repel the aggressor. On March 15, 2022, Dima turned 20. On the same day, he experienced the biggest battle of his life. At the beginning of summer, he became an artilleryman. On October 15, he was driving his SUV near the village of Sosnove in the Kramatorsk region, when he hit a landmine. Dima was at the wheel with his commander sitting beside him. The blast ejected him from the car, but he himself didn't feel it. He had lost consciousness. The passenger remained unharmed. He pulled Dima away from the burning vehicle. Used tourniquets to stop the bleeding from his torn legs. Dima regained consciousness, his commander went to seek help. An hour and a half later medics arrive. They came by foot along the railway tracks. This was the only safe way to reach Dima in the mined area. They carried him on a stretcher for about an hour along the railway tracks. Making their way to a vehicle that took Dima to the nearest village. There, he received initial medical aid. His first surgery was performed at a hospital in the Kharkiv region. Dima stayed there for a week. He was then transferred to a hospital in Sumy. Here he was met by his mother and father. Both of them come listen quietly beside their son when our conversation begins. When I ask Dima's mother Larissa about what had happened, she starts to cry.

The Poltava Orthopaedic Centre. The first prosthetics. Work to get used to them, to accept them. He also must accept the knowledge that he will never walk on his own legs again.

Dima is reticent, introverted. He responds to my questions very briefly. It creates a slightly uncomfortable feeling, but why should a young man open up to a stranger more than necessary anyway? I inquire about his plans for the future. He responds quickly. Dima says he's going back to the army. Back to his unit. The paperwork is in progress. Dima will become a squad leader, as his superiors have told him. Up until now, he has been a corporal.

His mother, standing nearby, tries to convince him that this idea is unfeasible. Dima remains determined. He knows several fighters who continue to serve despite losing a leg. Some without both legs as well. Dima communicates with them.

This young man is going back to the war. That's for sure. He's not going back merely to seek revenge on the enemy. He's drawn to the company of his comrades in arms. This pull back towards the war is something many frontline soldiers have described to me. It's a longing for a special camaraderie, strong bonds with the people alongside you.

Oksana

Do you remember the viral video on social media where a groom holds his legless bride in his arms? They're dancing the wedding waltz. That bride in the white dress is Oksana. I call Oksana, who's in Germany. She is in Hamburg with her husband and children. She is waiting for the completion of smart prosthetics. These are prosthetics with knees that can bend when walking. With these, Oksana will be able to walk on her own. Until then, she needs a rollator or crutches. But let's go back in time.

Oksana is a 25-year-old woman who worked as a nurse in the neurology department of the children's hospital in Lysychansk, Luhansk Oblast. Oksana and Viktor were young when they found each other and became parents. Their son Ilja is now 8 years old, and their daughter Diana is 6.

The war quickly and forcefully reached Lysychansk, located near Sievierodonetsk. The city is still under occupation. Little is left of it after the heavy bombings.

A year ago, on March 27, Oksana went with Viktor and a friend to pick up humanitarian aid. The streets were under fire from the Russians. It seemed safer to return through the summer cottage area along the river. Oksana walked slightly ahead of the men. At one point, she stopped. She turned to say something to Viktor. At that moment, a landmine exploded beneath her feet. Oksana fell face down but didn't lose consciousness. Viktor froze. He ran over, turned Oksana onto her back. He tore strips from his clothes to stop the bleeding. He called an ambulance. The ambulance refused to come until deminers had inspected the area and cleared it of mines. Viktor called Oksana's father. He ran to the scene. Viktor and Oksana's father carried her to the ambulance.

Oksana's mother also works as a nurse. When the ambulance brought Oksana to the hospital, her mother was waiting at the door. She knew what had happened. Oksana saw her, cried out "Mom!" and then lost consciousness.

Military doctors operated on Oksana. Most of the hospital's own doctors had already left the city by then. Oksana woke up from the anesthesia. She realised that her legs had been amputated above the knees. That was the moment when her will to live vanished.

On March 31, the family evacuated to Dnipro. They drove in two cars—Viktor and Oksana in the first, Oksana's mother, father, and the two children in the second. From Dnipro, Oksana was transferred to Lviv.

One day in April, Viktor told Oksana he was going out to buy water. Instead, he bought a ring. When he returned from the store, he put the ring on Oksana's finger. It was a marriage proposal, which Oksana accepted. On April 28, their wedding took place at the Lviv hospital. And the wedding waltz that the young couple danced, you must have seen.

How did the children react to the fact that their mother no longer had legs? Initially, when there was a blanket covering her lower body, they couldn't tell. When a wheelchair was given to

Oksana in Lviv, there were arguments between the brother and sister — both wanted to push their mother around in it. They probably shared that time equally.

The day came when Oksana and Viktor went to Germany to start the limb prosthesis process. The children remained with their grandparents for the time being. Diana told her brother that their mother would return from Germany with legs. Ilja realised that it wasn't exactly like that. He said that their mother would return with iron legs. Well, the main thing is that their mother starts walking.

Now, the family has been living together in Hamburg for almost a year. Oksana has received her initial prosthetics, and new ones with smart knees are in the making. When these smart-knee prosthetics are ready and Oksana learns to walk on them, she wants to return to Ukraine with her family. I ask Oksana if there's a chance that she'll have another child. She says she doesn't believe that will happen. First, she needs to get on her own two feet. And then help Diana and Ilja get on theirs.

Skeleton on a White Sheet

Oleksii is 37 years old. I ask him how many years he has been involved in searching for the remains of fallen soldiers. Twenty-four years is his reply.

Oleksii started doing this at the age of 13. Over the years, he and his companions found and excavated bodies belonging to soldiers who had fallen in World War II. Over three thousand Soviet soldiers, one thousand five hundred German soldiers. Among them were fifteen Estonians who fell in the ranks of the Waffen SS. Thanks to the efforts of Oleksii and his companions, many families found out the place of death of their fallen relatives and probably had then the opportunity to bury their remains in their local cemeteries back home.

The events of 2014 and the Russian invasion of Ukraine disguised as a separatist movement opened up a new dimension in Oleksii's work. Now he had to start searching for and identifying, if possible, the bodies of fallen soldiers on both sides of the conflict. The full on large-scale war has significantly increased the workload for him and other Cargo 200 employees.

I spend one long day with Oleksii and his team. They have received information about the remains of World War II casualties and about the remains of members of a Russian tank crew who died last summer. Life's paradoxes accompany the dead as well. That evening a Soviet soldier who fought against fascism in World War II and Russian soldiers who came to liberate Ukraine from its own people in 2022, were transported to the same morgue in the same vehicle, to await further examination.

A few months ago, one of the Cargo 200 vehicles maneuvered onto a landmine in the Kramatorsk region. One fatality. People injured. The rules for accompanying the group are strict. There's a whole squad of journalists. You must walk single file in each other's footsteps. Mustn't step off the path. The section of the road leading to the remains of the fallen has been cleared beforehand by deminers. We are in the vicinity of Bohorodychne. An area where major battles took place during World War II and last summer.

No war is fought with the dead. Oleksii and his associates do their work with extreme thoroughness and respect. Where I can only see a few pieces of bone lying by the road, Oleksii can immediately identify the location of the remains of the fallen. As a result of persistent and careful work, the skeleton begins to reveal itself. It is not a complete set, but each fragment, each piece of the skeleton is placed on a special white sheet onto which a delineation of the human skeleton has been drawn. The tibia set in its place, the finger bone in its place. The spine. Oleksii can instantly recognise which part of the skeleton each fragment is. The skull isn't found.

Hours of meticulous work and something resembling a human skeleton has appeared on the white vinyl surface. The soil is sifted through fingers to find even the tiniest fragments. A badge with a five-pointed star and a few buttons are found. Every stage of the work is documented with photographs, with tags bearing code numbers next to them.

Once everything has been documented, the findings are zipped up in a white body bag. Not once throughout the day do I witness any fragments being tossed aside. The men carefully pass each other even the smallest pieces from hand to hand. This isn't a façade, this is culture.

We move on, still single file. There's quite a bit of ground to cover. Along the same rutted road through some fields. An hour later, we reach the destroyed Russian tanks. Alongside the tanks are the remains of its members, who have been lying here since last summer, waiting to be recovered.

The same rules, the same stages. Determining the position of the remains, sifting through the fragments and placing them on the sheet. More personal items are found here of course. Nail clippers, a necklace with a Buddhist symbol. A partially burned pack of cigarettes with the warning *Smoking can kill*. A spoon, a small pack of tea. Some document—possibly a service contract.

A much more "complete" skeleton is forming on the white surface compared to the World War II victim. Understandable of course. Eighty years and nine months take a different toll.

Oleksii finds a bit of time to speak with me. He says that for him there are no "ours" or "theirs" among the dead. He believes that every family should have the opportunity to bury their fallen loved ones. He's a physical education teacher by education. He lost one of his eyes to a landmine explosion.

Our work often brings peace to mothers. Their sons get a grave in the local cemetery. This is a very important feeling and knowledge for the mothers. Two days ago in the nearby forest in Lyman, we found the remains of a 23-year-old Oleksandr. His squad was hit by an Uragan rocket in September. The remains of seven men were found, brought back and identified. Oleksandr was not among them. His mother contacted us. We went and found Oleksandr's remains. The explosion had torn him apart, and parts of his body were hanging from tree branches. His funeral is to be held soon.

It has started to rain. What I've written in my notebook smears and becomes partly illegible. Most of the journalists have already scattered. My fixer Sasha and I begin our journey back as well. Five kilometres of muddy field road lie ahead. Oleksii and his team stay behind to continue their work. I don't know how long it took them to finish the job. I doubt they made it home in daylight.

One day, the remains of these Russian fighters will be exchanged for the remains of Ukrainian soldiers found by the Russians. Bag for bag. Some mothers will finally be able to mourn — they will know their son has passed away and have a place to go to pay respect.

Sweet and Tender Beast

Sarmīte

People are preceded by stories about them. When I visited a sauna that was made in and sent from Estonia near Lyman in February, several people who I met there told me about a Latvian nurse. I didn't get to meet Sarmīte back then. She was out helping the wounded.

The day before yesterday, I was back again in the same place, at the same sauna. The sauna was intact and hot and some fierce fighters from Cuba had just stepped out of it. Upbeat, as people from there usually are. The sauna is still there, but quite a few people I met in February are not.

Sarmīte is still there. Warm, cheerful. She has an air of safety about her, like a loving mother surrounded by the many menfolk. Sarmīte recently received a medal of honor from the President of Latvia. She displays pride and dignity, but no arrogance.

When Sarmīte was a 14-year-old girl, she believed in science. What exists, is that which can be proven. One day she came home and said, "God, show yourself if you exist! My friend said you do".

And God gave a sign. Sarmīte does not specify how. She became a Christian, a priest as an adult, and a chaplain-soulkeeper. About her childhood, she says—it was tragic, difficult. A single mother had five daughters. Sarmīte being the oldest of them. Her stepfather was killed when she was 11. From then on, she became a second mother to her sisters.

Sarmīte was born near the Estonian border. Throughout her childhood, Estonian television was more accessible there than Latvian television. TV taught her a lot of Estonian. Sarmīte welcomes me in perfect Estonian. Heavenly Father, hello, meat, chicken, good morning—those are the words that first spring to her mind.

None of the wounded here have died in my arms, says Sarmīte. I've been able to stabilise them and send them on for further treatment. Wounded people behave very differently. Some scream, some are completely silent. Sarmīte has been wounded herself. It was a concussion and brain injury that sent her to the hospital for several weeks.

Any of us could be killed here, Sarmīte says. It's my time to be here right now. I'll die when it's time to die.

XXX7 and Bad Boy

Each fighter has their own call sign, a nickname. I meet a 42-year-old American, an experienced soldier with the call sign XXX7. When I ask him what the most difficult part of war is, he answers — immature, untrained soldiers that sometimes get sent to the front. We don't have time to train them here. They can't be trusted. Among them are irresponsible Instagram and TikToker soldiers. Such soldiers have uploaded videos to social media, on the basis of which the Russians were able to determine the exact destination of the attack. We sent them away.

How did you find the will to get here, I ask XXX7. We're fighting terrorists here, the man says. I don't want them in my country. I've had a life. I'm ready to die. But I can't watch from the sidelines as kids are being killed.

Bad Boy is a 21-year-old fighter from Colombia. "Very professional," as XXX7 describes him. Bad Boy inherited the nickname from his best friend with whom he came from Colombia to defend Ukraine. When his friend died, the young man took his name.

One key detail. An ad with a picture of Bad Boy has been circulated in Russian media, which promises $10,000 for killing the man in the picture. The picture can be viewed as "illustrative" — it calls for the killing of foreign soldiers fighting for Ukraine. I don't take pictures of these men. "We have a serious reason to avoid being famous," says XXX7.

Alexandra and Artur

Alexandra is in mourning. On April 9, her best friend was killed. Artur was the commander of the mortar unit. At 10:15 in the morning, a Russian missile fell on a house near the front where he was staying on the night of April 9. Artur was outside next to the house by his car. He was killed instantly. A pile of rubble stands instead of the house.

Alexandra's call sign is Little Flower. Her first commander gave her that name. Alexandra doesn't seem flower-like by nature. She gives the impression of being straightforward and decisive. She tries to be strong. It doesn't mask the mourning.

She's been in the battalion for a year already. She joined the ranks after seeing people get murdered by the Russians in Butcha. Started in the battalion as a drone pilot—observing the enemy territory, collecting information. She befriended Artur, who took her to his unit as an infantryman. Started learning to be a mortarman. Became Artur's aide. Now, after the death of her friend, she took command of the mortar unit. Temporarily, she thinks.

On the day that I meet Alexandra, Artur was buried in a graveyard near Kyjiv. Alexandra talks a lot about him. Artur is from Donetsk. His father is a high-ranking officer in the DNR. An officer who is fighting against Ukraine and who assured his son that Ukraine will soon give up. He invited his son to give up the fight. In response, Artur sent his father a photo where the middle finger of his right hand happened to be raised. His "personal" war was aimed at liberating his hometown of Donetsk from the occupiers.

Artur was absent-minded, forgetful, Alexandra says. I kept an eye on his things and doings at all times. He was like a pig—he kept getting dirty. I kept his uniform clean. He smashed cars. Once, when the car's engine stalled, he popped the hood and gently spoke to the engine. Closed the hood, turned the ignition—and the car started. His New Year's present to me was a protective vest.

On his helmet, Artur wrote the words *My Sweet and Tender Beast*. The helmet was now left in Alexandra's hands. *My Sweet and Tender Beast* is the Russian title for the feature film *A Hunting Accident* from 1978, based on Anton Chekhov's novel *The Shooting Party*. A film about a love triangle and its difficult conclusion.

Artur got married six months ago. We were friends, very good friends, Alexandra expresses. His body was burned, he was difficult to identify. It was confirmed based on a tattoo on his shoulder and chest. They were supposed to be flowers. Artur called them cabbages. A part of the tattoo was found under a charred layer. The night before, I asked Artur not to go to that house for the night. The house was targeted. The Russians had already sent four missiles nearby. He didn't listen to me.

Wedding Gowns in the Kramatorsk Morgue

Irina

Irina's mother passed away in 1998. In the morgue, there was no one to make sure she would be cleaned and dressed before being placed in a coffin. Irina went to the morgue, washed and dressed her mother. She did everything that one does to give a dignified farewell to the departed.

Her mother got sent off, but the experience stayed with Irina. Years later, Irina decided to go work in a morgue herself, to take care of the deceased. She went to work at the mortuary of a Kramatorsk hospital, where she has been working for 9 years. Irina is currently 51 years old. She's a junior nurse.

A year ago, on April 8, Russian forces fired on an evacuee train at the Kramatorsk train station. Sixty-one people died. Several of them were brought to the hospital's morgue. Not in one piece. Irina did everything she could to make sure that loved ones would and could be able to see the deceased before they were sent off. She placed the pieces of legs in a sheet and wrapped bandages around it to give the impression of a person with a leg. She mended broken skulls, patched up broken places and tied a bandage around it. One of the deceased stood out in Irina's memory. She was a young woman wearing a wedding dress. Irina did her best to prepare her for the farewell, as best as she possibly could. Did she make her beautiful? No, that can't be said.

In Ukraine, it's customary that when a young, unmarried girl dies, she is dressed in a wedding dress for her burial. One such dress is waiting on Irina's work table. Soon Angelica, a young woman is expected to be brought under her care. The bridal dress has already been prepared for her.

There are currently five deceased in Irina's morgue. An older man is on a stretcher near the door, a coffin is already waiting for him on the other side. Irina has placed a set of keys between his crossed fingers. These are the keys to the deceased's apartment, which his relatives will receive.

It may sound like an exaggeration, but I sense that Irina not only takes care of the deceased but also cares about them. She talks about them warmly and with respect. We stand and chat next to the deceased elderly gentleman. Irina's hand casually passes over the deceased's body and clothes. As if she's comforting him.

"I always silently wish a safe journey to those who are being taken away," Irina says. "I wish them wellbeing on the other side. May the earth receive them gently."

Viktoria and Aleksei

Victoria and Alexei are a married couple who make tombstones together. Their workshop is in the village of Ivanovka near Kramatorsk. When the war began, they left Donetsk and lived in Western Ukraine for a year with their 13-year-old son. They have now returned and resumed their work.

They met each other in Kamchatka, where Victoria was born and raised. Alexei moved to Kamchatka for work in 2009. The young couple met and stayed together. "When this war began, I felt ashamed of being Russian," says Victoria. Her relatives living near Kamchatka are increasingly becoming more distant. They don't understand what's happening here. "Russia didn't attack Ukraine," Victoria's mother tells her.

It's customary in Ukraine to engrave a portrait of the deceased and add a suitable phrase to their tombstone. Alexei shows a catalogue with hundreds of possible phrases to choose from. Here are a few that caught my eye. Engraving shorter sentences is, of course, cheaper than engraving longer ones:

"The warmth of your soul remains with us." — 95 hryvnia

"A big part of us went along with you. So much of you stayed with us." — 145 hryvnia

One elderly lady ordered granite crosses for her relatives' graves, thinking that when Resurrection Day comes, her relatives will be able to carry the crosses on their backs. She believed that those wouldn't be too heavy to bear. In reality, a granite cross doesn't weigh any less than a tombstone, says Alexei.

There are clients who aren't satisfied with the portrait engraved on granite, that has been made according to a photo. "Make them look younger. They smiled differently." Alexei and Victoria occasionally hear such requests. In their yard, stand some memorial stones that clients never picked up.

In the catalogue made for customers, there are sample photos using portraits of several actors. I recognise Stierlitz, meaning the Russian actor Vyacheslav Tikhonov.

There have also been Roma people among their clients. When a wealthy Roma baron passes away, they might get ordered a grandiose and detailed memorial stone. It could include, besides the baron, a costly mobile phone, money, a lavishly set table, and a thick gold chain around the baron's neck. Some people want there to even be a sandwich with red caviar, says Alexei. I believe that to be an exaggeration.

Sometimes, living people order memorial stones for themselves, and only the date of death needs to be added later. They then come and visit the workshop to see what they look like on the stone slab. "I've advised people not to order a memorial for themselves," says Alexei. "Let that be the concern of their loved ones."

One Grave, Two Trenches

Zoja

In the village of Rubtsy there's little life left. A few people are there who did not leave during the occupation. Most of the houses have been destroyed. There are so many wrecked houses in Donbass that the eye has become accustomed to it over the course of a week. You notice when there's a house that's intact. To your surprise.

Zoja's house stayed intact, but she herself is very broken. A year ago, on April 22, 2022 her son was shot and killed by the occupiers in their yard right before Zoja's eyes.

The village was under missile attack. Zoja and her son Alyosha had been taking cover in the basement all night. She had her icon with her there. Zoja prayed all night.

By morning, Rubtsy was occupied. Russian soldiers went house to house and checked who lived there. Zoja came out of the basement when she heard the voices of Russian soldiers. "Is there anyone else in there," they asked. "Come out, son!" his mother called out to Alyosha. Alyosha came.

Soldiers surrounded him in a semicircle. One of them, a buryat, saw tattoos on Alyosha's neck. A nationalist, a nationalist, he repeated. The buryat told the boy to get down on his knees and fired two bullets into his head. One came out of his eye, the other out of his throat.

The Russian soldiers left. Zoja was frozen in place for hours, sitting outside in the yard. She sat there, motionless. The sun started to set. She asked some neighbors to help. In the yard, in the garden bed, the neighbours dug a shallow grave. Maybe half a metre, not more, Zoja says. Alyosha was rolled into a carpet. For it to be softer for her son, Zoja put a couple of boards on the bottom of the grave with pillows on top. Her son was in the ground by the end of the day that he was murdered.

On November 22, Alyosha was moved and buried in a village graveyard. Alyosha has an older brother, Genya, who lives in Kramatorsk. Genya recently dreamed that a bordeaux-red rose should grow on the spot where Alyosha was first buried in their home garden.

I met Zoja on April 21. On April 22, exactly one year had passed since Alyosha was murdered. On that day, the older brother Genya came to his home village with his family, along with a bordeaux-red rose for planting. Right now, it should be about to blossom in the garden.

Nikolai

Trobyshevo village near Lyman. A man on the village street. Nikolai is his name. 58 years old. Says he's Hungarian by nationality and comes from Zakarpattia. I ask if he was living in the village when it was occupied. Yes, he was. And he tells me the story of his first contact with the occupiers.

In fact, the entire village was not yet in the hands of the Russians when it happened. Russian soldiers came to Nikolai's house and ordered him to go dig trenches. Nikolai refused. Also in the room were Nikolai's daughter and her daughter, 4-year-old Nazira. A Buryat soldier pushed the barrel of an automatic against the child's head. "Will you go dig?" Nikolai grabbed a shovel and went.

"I dug three or four shovel-fulls, threw the shovel down and came back home," says Nikolai. They never threatened him again.

Nikolai lives in his small house with his son-in-law Moissei. When they got the chance, his daughter and granddaughter Nazira left the village for Dnipro. Moissei was injured during the bombings. A blast threw him to the ground. Moissei fell and injured his knee on a brick. He had to lie in bed for three months. The knee needs surgery, but in Ukraine you have to pay for the operation. There's no money for that.

The barrel of the automatic aimed at the child's head left a mark. Nazira started stuttering.

Dima

24-year-old Dima is an experienced soldier. He went to defend Ukraine back in 2016 already. He was an artilleryman near Sievierodonetsk. He retired in 2019. Worked in Poland. On February 24, 2022, he was at work in Poland. On March 8, he returned to Ukraine. He started fighting under Kreminna. It's a rough area. Dima says you have to have balls of steel to fight there. He probably knows what he's talking about.

He talks about what happened a week ago. His tone is lively, figurative and humorous. What he's saying is not funny. All I can do is share fragments of it, because the whole story's just not there.

Dima's on the front lines with two of his comrades. A hundred or so metres of land separating them from Russian soldiers. You can hear them talking. Mortar fire. One of his companions loses his arm and leg. Dima drags him away, into a hole dug under a tree. Stops the bleeding. He hears the screams of another comrade at the front. "I'm 300!" 300 means being wounded. He gets to the comrade. His back is injured. He calls for his members of his unit to come help move away the wounded. At some point, he himself is able to return from the front. Twenty-four hours in the trenches, then a day's worth of rest. That's about the rhythm of the soldiers' life.

Surviving the front lines depends on how deep of a hole you can dig. The fighters are switched out at night. At night, you should also dig a hole as deep as possible and as soon as possible. "I dig for two or three hours without a break," Dima says.

A rest away from the front lines. Four actions done in the following order. Clean the automatic. Drink coffee. Take a shower. Sleep.

Do you remember where and when was the first time you killed an enemy? "I remember," Dima answers. "It was in 2018 under Zaitsevo. Our boys crawled to install mines. They came under fire from a machine gun. I shot at the machine gun. I saw him fall backwards. There was no feeling. I saved the lives of my companions. I don't count how many enemies I've killed. There should be more. The enemy must not be underestimated. You can't lose that sense of fear.

I could very well have stayed in Poland when the war broke out. I put together Teslas up there. I was earning well.

I want my loved ones to survive. That Mom and Dad could watch the parade in Kyiv on Victory Day. When you have a lot of money, there are a lot of people around you. When there's no money, your parents still remain. Always."

Dima has a 12-year-old sister, named Anna. A cheerleader who lives with their mother. For Anna's twelfth birthday, Dima sent their mother money to buy her sister an iPhone. Mom captured the moment when Anna got the gift. Dima shows me the video from his phone. A lovely girl at one moment starts spinning with joy. Her brother used his soldier's salary to pay for his sister's dream phone.

Dima checks the time. He will soon go back to Kreminna, back to his unit. Dad's taking him there. The few days of rest was over.

The Stunned People of Bakhmut

Kostiantynivka is an industrial city in the district of Kramatorsk. Bakhmut isn't far from here. The war is never far away in Donbas. A distant explosion woke me up the night before last. I woke up, listened. Today I found out that it was caused by a Russian rocket that hit a large building in Kostiantynivka, killing about ten people. One of the bodies hasn't been found yet. Those ten people died the moment when that explosion woke me up. They were also probably asleep but will never wake up again. I went back to sleep.

War refugees from Bakhmut have been brought to Kostiantynivka and they continue to be brought there. We go to one of the refugee accommodation centres. These people were brought here from Bakhmut, on the night of April 23. They are in a state of shock. They haven't emerged from the horrors yet that surrounded them for months. They do not wish to speak with journalists, and that's entirely understandable.

51-year-old Tetyana is helping war refugees, being a volunteer for the Stay Safe Ukraine organization. She's a war refugee from Bakhmut herself. She left in February. Her genuine concern and care for the newcomers arriving during the night is honest and immediate. She has asked many of them if they'd be willing to talk to journalists. The answer is no.

But Tetyana herself is willing. She finishes giving an interview to the Italian RAI news team. It's my turn.

She starts speaking in Ukrainian. I ask Tetyana if she'd be willing to speak to me in Russian. Of course, she responds. Russian is her first language. She switched to Ukrainian in February of 2022, when Russia attacked Ukraine.

We immediately find acquaintances in common. In Bakhmut, she was working alongside paramedics, including an Estonian. That of course being Erko Laidinen. Tetyana herself is a medic by education and profession—a nurse midwife. She didn't help deliver any babies during the war. She, however, saved the lives of many and was present during numerous killings and deaths.

The first wounded person whose life she managed to save — a woman lies on the street in a pool of blood, severely injured by shrapnel from a mine. Tetyana kneels down beside her, stops the bleeding with a tourniquet, stabilises her condition and hands her over to a team of paramedics. They take the woman to Kostiantynivka. From there, she's transported to a hospital in Dnipro. The woman survives.

Another woman didn't make it. She died in Tetyana's arms. Tetyana falls silent when she speaks of the realization that it was over. The blood flowing out of a person is still warm, but the person is gone.

A neighbour also dies. His name was Alexander Fyodorovich. We had just greeted each other with a raised fist — it means we'll persevere! A rocket strike. The neighbour is lying face down on the asphalt. Tetyana turns him over. His intestines hang out of his torn stomach. There are pieces of his kidney on the asphalt. The man still tries to gasp for air. Then he's gone.

Tetyana evacuated from Bakhmut in February of this year and immediately began setting up a refugee shelter in Kostiantynivka. She made trips to Bakhmut. She brought food and took people away from there. Her last trip was on February 27.

"It's hard to convince people to leave," she says. They live in basements, but these are basements close to home. Everything is still familiar. They lacked information regarding how they, as war refugees, would be treated. Whether their needs would be taken care of. Russian propaganda radio drowned out Ukrainian channels. Transistor radios constantly broadcast Russian appeals to "cross over", making assurances that they would be cared for. There were people with pro-Russian sentiments. Although, they all gladly accepted the aid brought by Ukrainians.

Tetyana tells of four women who fled Bakhmut on foot after their car had become inoperable. After ditching the car, it was hit by a shell. The last thing they did before leaving the car — let two guinea pigs out of their cage. They are still hoping that the guinea pigs managed to get away from the car. That they survived... These four women, ages 81, 50, 49, and 20, walked fourteen kilometres through a swamp, with mud up to their knees. Then they were noticed by Ukrainian soldiers. They brought the women to Kostiantynivka.

Tetyana tells us about Chechen fighters who fought for Ukraine in Bakhmut. One Chechen fighter told Tetyana, "We couldn't show Russia's true face to the world. Ukraine can!"

Tetyana has seen from aerial photos that her home in Bakhmut no longer exists. The garage is still there. Nevertheless, she wants to return to that city, her hometown, after its liberation.

I ask Tetyana if she's ever been to Estonia. She hasn't, but she has a mental image of Estonia. It's like a landscape with dollhouses. Everything is beautiful, orderly, and clean.

Do you have relatives in Russia? "I did, but not anymore. They no longer exist for me," says Tetyana. "When Russia attacked Ukraine, they started justifying Russia's aggression." From how many Ukrainians have I heard this from, I wonder...

No means no. I don't approach war refugees for interviews. But animals have nothing against communicating with me. I get to pet a dachshund. The dachshund's name is Semyon. Semyon sits at his owner's feet. The dog's sad eyes are on the lookout, to make sure the owner doesn't leave. When its owner briefly steps away, tears start to flow from Semyon's eyes. That's what the owner says and the same is confirmed by Tetyana.

There are also nine cats in the refugee shelter. I check them out as well. I remember two names. Manya and Barsik.

We begin to leave. There are three men standing outside. Are you from Bakhmut? Yes, we arrived during the night. Viktor, Oleg, Vladimir. Why did you stay there for so long? We were waiting for the Russians to be driven out of the city. Ukrainian fighters that we met in the city assured us that the city wouldn't be surrendered.

Cruel Jokes of War

Pavel shows me the driver's license of Noel, a U.S. citizen. Noel was born in 1996. He lived on Lincoln Avenue in New York. The license says he's a brown-eyed man. Five feet and six inches tall.

Noel WAS a man with brown eyes. He fell as a Wagner mercenary in Ukraine. The man who recently sent him to his grave with the fire of a machine gun was Pavel. It isn't very likely that Noel's body will ever make it back to his homeland. The Russians don't care about their dead — if the American mercenary can be counted as theirs. The bodies are left lying around, and now that the weather is warming up, it will be a real challenge for the Ukrainian fighters. Pavel says that if the bodies are 400-500 metres away, it's somewhat tolerable. Any closer than that and the stench is terrible. He knows what he's talking about. His second summer at war is about to begin.

Wagners fighting in Ukraine get paid 5,000 USD a month. The mercenaries are on a job. They are among the contracted Wagners from several countries. They have Kazakhs, Koreans. So Pavel assures me, having seen their bodies and documents up close.

Pavel is a 36-year-old Ukrainian soldier. Born and raised in Donetsk. In 2014, when the war began and the Donetsk pseudo-republic was declared, he came to Ukraine. Between 2014 and 2016, he defended Ukraine, fighting in Donbas. He retired on October 18, 2016. After giving birth to their daughter, Pavel's wife told him — choose, us or the war. You can't have both at the same time.

Pavel used to live and still lives with his family in Irpin, near Kyiv. On February 27, 2022, he and his comrades are already defending their hometown. "There were about a hundred of us," he says. "All former, experienced soldiers. We had few weapons. Two machine guns, two anti-tank weapons, automatics." On February 27, a convoy of Russian military equipment heads into the city. The defenders manage to destroy the unit at the head of the convoy. The rest retreat.

Butcha. A convoy of Russian military equipment consisting of two hundred units. "If they had made it to Kyiv, the city would have fallen in their hands," Pavel says. They didn't. Part of the convoy was destroyed, part of it retreated.

Miracles do exist. Pavel, along with seven comrades, rests in a two-story house in Irpin. A projectile with a radius of 152 millimetres falls on the house. The house collapses in a way that leaves an open space in the shape of a half-circle over the men downstairs. They are unharmed.

They move on to another house, its basement. The house sets on fire and the basement fills with smoke. The men leave and immediately after that, a projectile falls on this house as well. The basement is also destroyed. The smoke saved the men. "All eight are still alive and well," Pavel says.

The last battle in Irpin. The Russians are retreating. In the morning, Pavel goes to assess the situation. A soldier sits by the Russian BMP (infantry fighting vehicle). Pavel aims at him. Tells him to put his gun down. "Don't shoot," the Russian pleads. Pavel takes him to his unit.

The man Pavel captures is later traded for a Ukrainian prisoner. Timofei Babov is the name of this Russian. He's a champion athlete in boxing. He came to Ukraine as a mercenary to lay the groundwork for his further career as a boxer. The status of a military veteran would have led to advantages when becoming a professional boxer.

Pavel stayed in touch with Timofei on social media. Still does. Timofei was greeted in Russia as a traitor of his homeland, a surrenderer. He's under constant surveillance, occasionally taken to interrogation. Nothing has changed in that country.

In Irpin, Pavel runs for forty minutes on the heels of a Russian fighter until he gets a chance to kill him. The Russian fighter had a backpack full of men's underwear stolen from a store. Pavel makes no secret of the fact that he still has some left to use. Later, I hear that Pavel is a former marathon runner.

A lot of strange, tragic and grotesque stories can be heard from Pavel. An explosive is dropped onto an occupier by drone. In the video we can hear the drone operator's voiceover: "This video of the killing of the enemy is dedicated to so and so". The use of a drone is part of everyday war, but providing commentary over the footage is commissioned. Necessary equipment can be purchased with the money received from the order. Pavel has sent several bags of trophies collected in the war to be auctioned abroad. For the money he got, he bought the jeep that I took his photo with.

The village of Dementjevka near Kharkiv. Pavel talked a lot about protecting it last summer. It was a long and rough battle that little is known about. Dementjevka is located on the highlands. If Russians had captured it, it would have been much easier for them to bomb all of Kharkiv. They didn't take it.

Piece by piece, fragments of this long defensive battle are collected. Two thousand projectiles a day fall on the village. Many dead and wounded. An arm that's been torn off a body is lying on the ground. "I knew whose it was," Pavel says. Water scarcity. You stop by a fallen comrade to pour the water from his canteen into your own. Anton, a comrade going into battle is without a helmet. Pavel lend him his own and asks him to bring it back later. Anton calls him later, asks if he can keep the helmet. It saved his life. Two pieces of shrapnel hit the helmet, but the man was unharmed.

One time Pavel goes to Kharkiv. His comrades write down their partners' phone numbers and text messages on paper. Pavel, who reaches cell service in Kharkiv, sends them along to the women from his phone. *I'm fine. Love You.*

People joke around during war as well. Laughs are had. Otherwise, you would probably go crazy. Some do.

The same Dementjevka near Kharkiv. Russians have surrounded the village. Pavel sends an SMS to the commander of the Russian unit facing them. We'll give up if you pay every man 50,000 USD. The Russians take the offer seriously and are ready to talk trade. These "negotiations," however, never get anywhere.

Ukrainian fighters know that the Russians are listening to their radio communication. So they feed them false information. "Myhhail, our tanks are approaching. A hundred men are joining you on the left flank." Soon enough there's hustle and bustle on the Russian side. They're relocating their resources to "where there'll be men and tanks." The Russians are left waiting, because they were never there nor were they ever coming.

Still in Dementjevka. A night-time view through a thermal camera. A four-man group of Russians is moving — one after the other. The last one keeps falling behind. The first one tells him to catch up. He does. Then falls behind again. The first one turns back and shoots the last one. The men then move on, with no more falling behind. That the kind of men they are.

Pavel's parents and older brother live in Russia. Pavel doesn't have many kind words to say about his brother Dima. He just tells the truth. My brother's a dollar millionaire. A businessman who now went into politics. On the side of United Russia, of course. This gives him a better chance to get a hold of contracts related to the supplying of the army. When Russians occupied Kherson, the brothers made a bet with each other — whether Mykolajiv will be occupied or not. Brother Dima said they will occupy. Pavel said they won't. The loser would have to buy their father a new car. Dima bought it. Not like that was any kind of a notable expense for a dollar millionaire.

Pavel and I met in Kostyantynivka. He's gotten a little vacation. He went home to see his wife and daughter in Irpin. Now he's waiting for the order to go back to the front. I don't see cruelty or any desire to kill in his eyes. He's a soldier. He protects his land for as long as he needs to. As long as he can and will. Then he'll return to his normal life. In order to retain strength of spirit, you have to sometimes joke around during war. Some of these jokes can be very cruel. But war itself is even more cruel.

Wagner Captives in Dnipro Prison

Visiting the prison before leaving Donbas is becoming a habit for me. I met three Russian pilots there in February. They of course had only bombed empty fields and abandoned buildings before ending up in prison. Not a single person was killed or injured by their bombs. Guaranteed.

After our interview in February, the pilots asked whether I had any cigarettes or chocolate for them. I didn't. Now, at the end of April, I bought several packs of cigarettes to bring with me. I thought maybe a guard could pass them on to the pilots. But the pilots were already free men. They were exchanged for Ukrainian fighters a couple of weeks ago. I hope they're at home, reunited with their wives and children. And they can suck on their cigarettes as much as they please.

Remember when I recently wrote about a Ukrainian war prisoner in the Voronezh Oblast's prison who got a plate of lousy porridge as his daily food ration. Who wasn't allowed to sit during the day, let alone lie down. If he would, he'd be beaten. Who could once per month only spend half an hour outside in the fresh air. It seems to me that compared to the suffering Ukrainian soldiers in Russian prisons, the Russian war prisoners in Ukraine are like living in a sanatorium. But still not a sanatorium I would want to end up in.

The prison wasn't completely empty of Russian war prisoners. Even though about a couple dozen Wagner private army soldiers were exchanged a few days ago, two of them remained unexchanged. Plus a soldier-separatist from the Luhansk People's Pseudo-Republic. It is with them that I meet at noon on April 25.

Genghis

I'm not sure whether 25-year-old Genghis carries any of Genghis Khan's genes. It's widely known that there are a lot of people in the world who carry it. In the territories of the former Mongol Empire alone, about eight percent of men carry on his genes. It's a paradox of history that the murderers of millions become prominent figures, while the killers of a few remain just killers.

Genghis is just a killer. He visited his sister a couple of years ago in the Russian city of Tyumen. She studied to become a nurse there, maybe she continues to do so to this day. Genghis didn't elaborate on the details, but in an altercation, one of his male acquaintances started making advances toward his sister, behaving indecently with her. Genghis stepped in to defend his sister's honour. He told me he struck the offender, causing him to fall and hit his head. He was taken to a hospital where he died. The exact turn of events remains unknown to me.

Genghis was sentenced to ten years in a Russian prison. He spent a couple of years in a penal colony in the Tyumen Oblast. In October 2022, a recruiter from the Wagner private military company arrived at the colony. Two hundred inmates chose a career as mercenaries over long prison sentences. In return, they were promised a salary, amnesty after six months of fighting in Ukraine, or death. As did everyone else, Genghis believed he would survive and receive amnesty after six months. He signed the contract with the Russian Ministry of Defence, not with the Wagner private army. This is important information. How did the colony contribute to the inmates' decision-making? Sometime before the recruiters arrived, the inmates' living conditions deteriorated even further. The food became worse, the regime stricter.

A couple of weeks of training in Rostov. Each man is assigned a pseudonym using a computer program. Genghis' pseudonym was Propil. In English it would probably translate to propyl. Which should be the food preservative E217.

Up next Luhansk. The contract criminals have been told that the punishment for consuming alcohol and drugs, commiting looting or rape, is execution. In Russian, there is a euphemism used for this—"абнулить". "Zero out". Around seven hundred contract criminals were lined up in a square in Luhansk. Two men who had violated these rules were brought before them and executed. "Zeroed." They were given the opportunity to say their last words beforehand. There were two executioners, just like there were two being executed.

121

In early December 2022, Genghis was taken with his fellow Wagner mercenaries to positions near Kreminna. From there over to the Soledar region. They were ordered to advance to an area that was purportedly already in the hands of "their side." It wasn't. Ukrainian units were there. I don't know how many of them survived, but Genghis was captured there. Without a battle, he claims.

Genghis' future appears bleak. He'll probably be exchanged for a Ukrainian prisoner at some point. Returning to Russia wouldn't mean freedom or release. The contract wasn't fulfilled. Instead of six-months, he only spent a few weeks on the front lines. One of the possible scenarios is that he'll just be executed. "Zeroed" somewhere in the wilderness or on an empty field. Or will he be sent back to serve the remainder of his sentence in the Tyumen colony? Or maybe he'll be extradited to Kazakhstan, where a lengthy prison term awaits him for his involvement in Wagner's private army.

Has Genghis seen the video showing the execution of Yevgeni Nužin with a sledgehammer, a defector from Wagner's group. Yes, he's seen it here in the Dnipro prison.

Genghis himself doesn't believe that he would be killed upon return to Russia. He says there are too many people who know where he has been. He clings to hope. He wants to return home, to Kazakhstan, to the city of Pavlograd. To his parents. He wants to continue working as a truck driver. Genghis has a 5-year-old son named Ruslan, whom he hasn't seen in a long time. In 2021, his father visited him in prison. His parents are unaware of his involvement with Wagner, only his sister knows.

I give Genghis a pack of cigarettes, I have nothing more to give.

Andrei

Andrei is the first separatist who I saw face-to-face. That is, if we leave aside those civilians who, while living in territories of Ukraine under Russian bombardment, are still longing for a Russian world. That's because the slave mentality of the Russian world is so deeply ingrained in them that even Russian bombs are seen as their own and lovely. A few days before my visit to the prison I met one such person in a village near Lyman, a place bombed to pieces by the Russians. The Anglo-Americans are to blame, they started the war, an old man told me in the village shop. The Russians pre-empted the planned attack to protect themselves from Ukrainian fascism.

Andrei is feeble and pathetic. Someone who's ready to obey any order to ensure his own survival. He joined the Luhansk separatist army in 2021. His teeth were and still are unfortunately in very poor condition. Andrei became a mercenary to get new teeth. The salary would have made that possible. Initially, he was paid 18,000 roubles a month. Then 24,000 and finally 78,000 roubles. Although he didn't get the chance to buy new teeth. He was captured beforehand.

Every frontline soldier has a pseudonym. Andrei is a football fan whose favourite team is Manchester United. He chose Maradona as his pseudonym. He however gave himself a black eye somehow — or was given one. And the battalion commander began calling Andrei "Sinjak" — "Bruise". Andrei would've liked to be Maradona but got stuck with Sinjak instead and couldn't get rid of it.

In June 2022, Andrei was sent to the front line with his unit. The period from June to September remains confusing. One thing is clear — he hasn't killed anyone. Place names mentioned include Bilohorivka, Vrubivka, Spirne. On September 1, Andrei was captured near the village of Spirne, Bakhmut district. He was afraid that the Ukrainians would shoot him on the spot.

Andrei gradually realises his mistakes. He found the formation of the LNR incomprehensible. He didn't vote in favour of it during the referendum. Andrei had studied Ukrainian at school. Taras Shevchenko's poem "Sleep" had become especially dear to him. He just needed new teeth and that's why he went to war.

In the strict regime prison where Andrei awaits his fate, he is given three meals a day. On the morning of our meeting, he had eaten porridge. For lunch he had soup and porridge with meat. He is allowed outside for a walk every day. Time passes by slowly. Prisoners can borrow books. Andrei has read fifty books in half a year. He's currently finishing Arthur Conan Doyle's *The Lost World*.

Andrei exits the room into the corridor. A guard comes and warns us not to allow the prisoners to leave the meeting room by themselves. Russian war prisoners have reason to fear Ukrainian "zeks" — criminals. In prison, it is ensured that they don't come into contact with one another.

I give Andrei a pack of smokes. That's all I have to give him.

Ruslan

Ruslan is a 42-year-old Tatar who was recruited into Wagner from Correctional Colony No. 1 in Chelyabinsk, notorious for its strict regime. Ruslan was a drug addict who had been sentenced for drug-related crimes. He had served a year and a half of his ten-year sentence when he was offered to become cannon fodder in the war. Ruslan didn't hesitate for long. He suffers from AIDS. Doctors have given him a life expectancy of three to four years. He wouldn't have returned from prison alive anyway.

Ruslan got married at a young age. His daughters, Yana and Anna, are already 24 and 21 years old. His daughters have done well. They're studying at a college. They lost their mother when they were in kindergarten. She was only 23 years old. "I was preparing to take the kids to kindergarten in the morning," says Ruslan. "My wife hadn't gotten up for some reason. I went to check on her. She had died in her sleep. Her heart had stopped".

Ruslan used to work as a carpenter and raised his daughters. He tried drugs for the first time about ten years ago. He started shooting up and was hooked.

On January 10, 2023, Ruslan, alongside other new Wagner recruits, was flown to the Rostov training ground. He underwent three weeks of training. He along with other fresh recruits were then taken in the back of a Kamaz truck to Bakhmut. Seven days later, on February 11, Ruslan was wounded in combat and taken captive. He got shot in the arm and leg. His life was saved by the assault rifle behind his injured arm, which prevented the bullet from penetrating further into his body.

A day spent in a garage with two fellow captives. His wounded arm had been sealed off with a tourniquet, to stop the bleeding. It was left on the arm for the entire day. When medics removed it in the pre-trial detention centre, his hand was already dead. Its tissues had been irreversibly damaged.

Ruslan doesn't know what awaits him after a prisoner exchange. Getting "zeroed out"? It's a possibility. His daughters are of great importance to him. That is evident. Ruslan's mother is aware of her son's whereabouts. They have exchanged a couple of letters through the Red Cross.

I give Ruslan two packs of cigarettes. One for himself and the other to be shared among the three, with one third for Genghis and one third for Andrei.

Anatoly's One Hundred Days of Torture

Sergei, a friend living in Kharkiv, told me about Anatoly. Anatoly is a seventy-year-old filmmaker who lives in the Savyntsi settlement of Balakliia district of Kharkiv Oblast. He started filming in 1976. Trying to count all the stories he's captured on film over the decades would be impossible. In the beginning he used 35mm film and for the last thirty years he's been recording digitally. For Anatoly, being a filmmaker was his bread and butter. However, it could have cost him his life in the spring of 2022.

Anatoly has filmed and posted about five hundred videos on his Youtube channel. He is like a chronicler of his area, whose films could easily be the basis for a doctoral thesis of some anthropologist. There are so many videos and I only managed to watch a few. One caught my eye and stayed with me.

The May 9th celebrations of 1995 in Savyntsi. A theatricised procession. A cardboard Brest fortress on the back of a truck, lined with actual verdant birches. Soviet soldiers sit inside the fortress and hang from it as well.

A line of weeping women, dragging their feet, walk by. Everyone is wiping their eyes with the corner of their headscarf. Why are they crying? A fascist walks into frame, who is convoying these women. An automatic, a German soldier's uniform. Everything as it should be.

The back of the truck has a wire fence built all around it. There are prisoners behind the fence in striped prison garb. Like a little slice of concentration camp.

Lathes with machinists working on them — all in the back of the truck. *All for the front! All in the name of victory!* is written on the side of the vehicle. They're probably producing projectiles in that truck.

A truck bed filled with a bunch of sand. Soldiers with shovels. Installing a border pillar with the letters *CCCP* (USSR). What year could this be? Is it 1939, when the MRP secret protocols divided Poland up between the two aggressors?

This video, shot in 1995, is meaningful. Ukraine's independence, its self-reliance is still in its infancy. It's identity is blurry, especially in eastern Ukraine. The crimes of German fascism are vividly remembered, unlike those of Russian communism. It is interesting to observe how the stories told through Anatoly's videos reflect growing up Ukrainian, becoming Ukrainian throughout the decades. How Ukrainian replaces Russian at school assemblies. How blue and yellow start to wave instead of red.

I call Anatoly. Cell service is poor, but we manage to talk. He begins his story from 2014, when before the full blown war, there was a long pre-war underway. Anatoly delivered aid packages as a volunteer to Ukrainian units made up of volunteers. He recorded videos of what was taking place on the front lines.

The first days of full blown war. Already on March 2, 2022, Russian forces occupy Savyntsi. At six o'clock in the morning, Anatoly films a convoy of Russian troops passing by the window of his home. Uploads the footage to the internet. Yet takes it down on March 6.

Anatoly gives the Ukrainian troops information on the location and movement of Russian troops by phone. He coordinates the fire, so to speak.

On March 10, someone from his settlement calls him. Threatens him. He is surrounded by many individuals who could and would betray him. "There are a lot of supporters of the "Russian world" in Savyntsi," Anatoly says.

Anatoly senses the danger. He moves from his apartment to a nearby cottage. On May 28, they come for him. The first beating. Anatoly is taken to his apartment. They search it and take his equipment with them. The first interrogation in the Savyntsi' City Council garage. The second beating.

He's tied up and subjected to electric shock torture. He loses consciousness. "If they had known I was coordinating the attacks, they would have shot me on the spot," says Anatoly. "But they only knew about the videos."

Anatoly is taken to Balakliia, the district centre. He's put in isolation in a basement. During the first three days they carry out eight interrogations. Each interrogation lasts two hours. The interrogator tortures him with electric shocks. But the Russians aren't only skilled in designing torture devices. They also have innovative methods for teaching Russian. Speaking in Ukrainian, each word uttered in Ukrainian leads to an electric shock for Anatoly. The interrogator calls the process a Russian lesson.

Fellow prisoners. They change from time to time. Maksim from the neighbouring cell is shot. The Russians had information that he was coordinating fire. Maksim's body will be handed over to his mother.

There's blood on the wall of the interrogation chamber. A bullet from a pistol is lodged in the wall. What did the interrogators want? "They wanted me to work for them," said Anatoly. "Asked me to start making propaganda videos for them." Anatoly refused.

One day, they tell Anatoly to prepare for his death. "You will be executed in one hour," the Russian says. That's when Anatoly falls silent. I can tell that he's holding back tears. They didn't come in an hour. They didn't even call him in for questioning for three whole weeks. An hour of intense fear was extended to three weeks. No one, in those three weeks, told Anatoly that he wouldn't be shot. Which meant that a terrible fear arose in him, every time his cell door was opened. Were they coming for me?

Twice a day, in the morning and in the evening, the prisoners are taken out of the basement with bags put over their heads. Ten minutes for going to the bathroom. The cell becomes suffocating for Anatoly — the other convicts smoke.

The occupiers released Anatoly on September 4. He had been in captivity for a hundred days. The Russians were in a hurry — on September 7, Ukrainian troops were already in Balakliia. When a long-bearded Anatoly reached home on September 4, Savyntsi was still occupied. But as early as September 13, Anatoly borrows a video camera from a friend and goes to Balakliia to collect footage. On September 16, he is in liberated Izyum. This is the time when the bodies of people executed by the Russians are exhumed from under a pine forest close to the city. Anatoly happens to be on a bus that has brought ten foreign journalists to Izyum. When they find out the story of his imprisonment, all ten of them want an interview with him. All ten promise to send him the published story. Anatoly is still waiting for those ten published stories.

"But I will send you my story," I promise Anatoly. And I did, too. Really.

Auntie Lehte from Popilnia Village

I was four or five years old. I got to feed calves with milk. I believed I was doing it as a job. I was paid three roubles for it. Those were my first earnings and feeding calves was my first job. I watched a pig being castrated. I was scared of an angry rooster outside who jumped on top of my head a couple of times. I gave a piece of sugar to a horse from the palm of my hand. I tugged on a cow's udder, hoping that milk would start to trickle. It didn't. I buried the base of an old copper-coloured petroleum lamp in the sand. It's my hidden treasure, waiting to be dug out for over fifty years.

The mean rooster ended up in a soup pot. I stuck one of his feathers in my hair and I became an Indian. The last Mohican, of course. I had a bow. During those summers I felt fully alive, as children do.

All of this happened at aunt Lehte's place in Nõva, Estonia. Aunt Lehte had a husband but didn't have any children. I probably filled a gap in her longing for a child. For the sake of simplicity, I call her Aunt Lehte. Lehte is technically my cousin.

Aunt Lehte grew up as an orphan. On June 25, 1941, forest brothers in Võru County shot her father, who had gone along with the Soviet occupation. It had been less than two weeks since the brutal day of the June deportation when tens of thousands of people from Estonia were deported to Siberia and sent to the Gulag. Lehte had just turned four a couple of days before her father's death. In 1946, her mother died after being hit by a car.

The August storm of 1967 brought down trees and bent the fate of people. A significant number of Ukrainians came to Estonia to work in the storm-damaged forests. Among them was a young, hot-blooded man named Aleksander. I don't know exactly how or where it ignited, but Lehte's love for Aleksander took her to Ukraine. My childhood summers in Nõva came to an end.

Years became decades. I knew that somewhere far away in Ukraine, in the Zhytomyr Oblast, Aunt Lehte was living her life. How she was living it, I did not know.

This time I drove to Ukraine with my own car. I reached the Zhytomyr Oblast two days ago. I called someone in Estonia who I thought might know more about the fate of aunt Lehte. I got the name of the village — Popilnia. I also learned that Lehte had passed away in 2019. I already knew that Lehte had an adopted daughter named Ilona.

Two hours of dodging potholes. It's a large village. I started at the village council. Maybe somebody there knows someone who might have known Lehte.

I meet with the secretary of the village council. I'm so and so, inquiring about Lehte. Lehte — the midwife? Yes, she also worked as a medic in Estonia. But she's dead... Dead? No, Lehte is alive. If you go past the church, take the second street across the road. The first two-story house. That's where she lives with her daughter and her daughter's husband. Yes, Lehte's husband Aleksander died already back in 2003.

Mykhailo, Lehte's son-in-law, arrives. I follow him in my car. We enter the house. Mykhailo opens the door to one of the rooms. In bed lies a petite elderly woman. It's 85-year-old Lehte, who I remember as a very young woman. I sit down beside her. Hello, Lehte! I am Vahur. A glimmer of recognition in Lehte's eyes. She replies in fluent Estonian, without an accent. We talk. Lehte sometimes switches to speaking in Russian. She speaks softly and intermittently. I don't understand all of it. But she is cognisant, she understands and remembers. "My homeland is Estonia", says Lehte. Her eyes fill with tears. Do you want to be buried in Estonia, I ask. Yes. Lehte wants to be buried in the Pindi cemetery — in the family burial plot where her father, mother and grandmother rest. My mother as well.

Ilona arrives, Lehte's 43-year-old daughter. We talk to her about the fact that Lehte is not her biological mother. Ilona's biological mother, being a young 18-year-old woman, abandoned her right after her birth in the maternity hospital. Lehte started taking care of the abandoned baby. The newborn remained in the maternity hospital for seven months before Lehte could bring her home.

I go to Lehte once more. I tell her that she is a very dear and important person to me. Those summers spent at her home in Nõva are still with me. I ask Ilona to take a photo of us. I leave. I feel I have finally closed a chapter that had been unresolved for over fifty years. I got to thank Lehte and say goodbye.

The Liberation of the Azovstal Doctor

Olyksandr is a thirty-two-year-old anesthesiologist. In 2016, he was already working as a doctor in Mariupol. Lest we forget—Russia's aggression in Ukraine began in 2014. In every major village in Ukraine, not to mention in every city, there are memorial plaques with pictures of the men and women who were lost between 2014 and 2021. There were many.

On February 23, 2022, Olyksandr got a call with orders to be prepared for the outbreak of a large-scale war. The first wounded to be brought to Dnipro Military Hospital, where he was working at the time, arrived at around five o'clock on the evening of February 24.

On the night of March 31, a helicopter takes off from a Dnipro airfield with Olyksandr on board, along with another anesthesiologist, two surgeons and a nurse. The helicopter is chock full of medical equipment. The helicopter is headed to Mariupol—a city already in ruins by then. They take a longer route, flying above the sea.

At around five o'clock in the morning, the helicopter lands in the port of Mariupol and immediately falls under missile fire. They unload the equipment from the helicopter and place in it the wounded who had been brought there by car. It takes a while for the medics to reach the Azovstal steel plant. The following night they move on by motorboat. They're met halfway. A huge air strike to the factory's grounds. Huge? What would even be the right word to use?

Including those who just arrived, twenty-five medics are working in the hospital in Azov territory. Together with those who arrived, there are five surgeons and four anaesthetists. They are able to work above ground until March 16. Then the hospital is hit and destroyed. The work is continued in the basement of the plant.

His first patient? He was a fighter with a severe shrapnel wound in his arm. The arm was saved, it didn't have to be amputated.

I can only relay fragments of what Olyksandr said. My perception, my interpretation of his life and work under constant bombardment. The longest shift Olyksandr has worked without rest is thirty hours. Throughout their time in Azovstal, medics are able to save the lives of about four hundred fighters. Medical supplies and medicines are becoming increasingly scarce. The dead are placed in refrigerators, which can still be kept cool with the help of generators.

We were ready to die, says Olyksandr. On April 28, a three-ton fougasse bomb falls on the factory. Surviving that is a miracle. Olyksandr is thrown eight metres by the blast. He gets a severe concussion.

Not once did Olyksandr leave the basement from April 3 to May 16.

On May 16, they begin surrendering. First, the badly wounded. They all exit in small groups. Olyksandr leaves the basement on the evening of May 18 with a group of fifteen medics. The captors divide those exiting into three groups right away. Fighters from the Azov battalion, women and officers separately. Prisoners are convoyed onto buses. Anyone who moves or turns around too much will be killed on sight, the prisoners are told.

The journey to Yelenovka, to the 120nd colony near Donetsk, which was already closed down a few years ago. The imprisoned are divided into barracks. Around each barrack there is a small zone where one can move in. You're not allowed outside it. The DNR's so-called separatists take everything there is to take away from the prisoners. Olyksandr loses his flashlight and headphones. He already destroyed his phone before leaving the basement. But prior to that he was able to send a few photos of his work via Starlink. And those are added to this story here.

Medics who were on the territory of a factory called Illich in Mariupol were imprisoned as early as April. They — those who are still alive — are in the same camp. They have been badly beaten, one of the wounded among them was said to have been beaten to death.

The prison guards are extraordinarily cruel and extraordinarily stupid. The majority of them represent Russian ethnic minorities. The prisoners are convoyed to Donetsk for questioning by 18 to 20-year-old DNR "fighters". Thanks to his medical background, Olyksandr recognises them to be drug addicts. What is more, some of them even spoke fluent Ukrainian, says Olyksandr. You weren't allowed to raise your head in the convoy. That led to a hit on the head with the butt of an automatic.

"I can't talk about the torture," says Olyksandr. He's not the first imprisoned combatant I've met. There are things none of them can talk about. Not yet. That time will come.

Psychological tactics, brainwashing. Life with constant Russian music. The prisoners are assured that Kyiv is already in the hands of the Russians. You get "food" three times a day. Water that has a few cabbage leaves and pieces of potato floating in it. "Stone" porridge—some kind of unprocessed and uncleaned grain onto which water has been poured.

Drinking water is brought with fire engines from a nearby river. Consuming it causes serious digestive problems for many.

Olyksandr's weight before captivity was 120 kg. After captivity it was 76 kg. He lost 44 kg.

Four hundred and sixty prisoners were placed in the barracks at first. Some slept on the concrete floor. Later, there were fewer of them. There were wounded too. From time to time, they brought bandages. The medics changed the bandages of the wounded.

On July 29, Olyksandr sees four Grad rockets being placed near the bordering fence of the camp. At around eight or nine o'clock in the evening, they start shooting towards Marinka. At the same time, explosions can be heard from one of the camp's barracks. The prisoners are forbidden to leave the barracks.

That's a barrack where about 200 Azov Battalion fighters are stationed. It is mass murder. The shooting from the Grad rockets was meant to cover the sound of explosions from the barrack. Fifty-three of the prisoners in the barrack died immediately or of the wounds sustained. That may not be the exact number. It wasn't until midnight that medics went to the barrack to find the wounded. They waited four hours, giving those people time to die, people who might otherwise have survived if aid had been administered sooner.

In the morning, the wounded were loaded onto Kamaz trucks from the barrack. Olyksandr remembers their screams. Loaded up like meat, he says.

When did you feel the most fear, I ask. The answer is surprising. Or maybe not. The worst fear was when we were loaded onto a plane, says Olyksandr. When we realised we were being traded for Russians. I was afraid the plane would be shot down.

The flight first was to Moscow, then to Belarus. For two whole days, no one is allowed to the toilet. Buses take them to the exchange zone. Crossing the border along trench lines. At some point—the realization that you're in your home country. Amongst your own people. That you're alive.

"My parents only found out when watching TV that I was in Azovstal and later in captivity," says Olyksandr. "I didn't want them to worry."

"One patient, who was already clinically dead, I had to resuscitate three times. His arm and leg were crushed. I was afraid he wouldn't survive. On May 16, he was taken away—to prison. When I was on TV after I was released, he recognised me and contacted me. That was a great joy. And the hand and the leg were saved!"

Estonian Body Armour and Bullets in Gunya's Body

I draw a person wearing a vest in my notebook. I ask Gunya to mark on it where the impact points of the bullets were that penetrated his hand, hit his phone and his plate carrier vest. The one that got stuck in his back. We meet in a village near Zaporizhzhia. Gunya is a pseudonym. Gunya is a 47-year-old fighter named Andrey, from a village near Lviv. He's a member of the Ukrainian Nationalist Battalion (OUN).

Gunya has survived thanks to an armoured vest brought from Estonia, bought with money gathered by Estonians. Battle for the village of Pobjeda near Marinka. For Gunya, the fight ends on February 22, 2023. He is severely wounded. Ukrainian units liberate the village of Pobjeda by February 24, just in time for the first anniversary of the ongoing war.

Gunya describes what happened. He is entering a basement that he thought was empty, already "cleared out." He's standing at the top of the stairs. Suddenly, he's staring down the barrels of two assault rifles. The distance is three metres. It takes a second for Gunya, using the arm bands for reference, to determine if they are friendly or enemy soldiers. Then the guns do the talking. Probably almost simultaneously from both sides. Gunya loses consciousness. When he regains consciousness, he reaches for his assault rifle. He tries to fire it. No shots follow. Near Gunya lies his fellow fighter who has been wounded. Gunya strains to reach his comrade's rifle. Manages to get a hold of it. Slightly lifts himself up and fires a steam of bullets into the basement. He thought his own weapon had jammed. It hadn't. The magazine was empty. At the same time as he was being hit by Russian bullets, Gunya managed to empty his weapon in their direction. Killing them. Sometimes referred to as *obnulitj* in Russian. *To zero.*

Heavy bleeding from his fractured arm. One leg is immobile. Gunya applies the first tourniquet himself with his uninjured arm.

It takes about an hour for help to arrive. A medic puts another tourniquet on his wounded arm. Gunya leaves. He is taken to a car. Surgeries and rehabilitation follow, with a long road toward recovery only halfway through.

How many bullets and where did they hit Gunya? One bullet entered from the left side of his vest, which wasn't covered by the metal plates and got lodged in one of his back muscles. Another one pierced Gunya's phone which was in his pocket. The phone could be regarded as the second lifesaver besides the vest. The bullet then changed its direction and only grazed his stomach, instead of penetrating his body. Two bullets went through his left arm, shattering bones, before deflecting off his body armour. The fifth bullet pierced Gunya's left pocket, destroying his documents, but did not penetrate his body.

We talk in a first aid bus, which was also provided by Estonians. Gunya digs out the body armour from the back of the bus. Its plates were imported from Estonia. Gunya had already replaced the textile "shell" before being wounded. Not that there was anything wrong with the Estonian one. It's just that his friend Igor gave him another shell as a gift, so Gunya switched the plates over. A gift from a friend, after all. The vest bears bloodstains and two bullet holes. The holes are only in the fabric. The plates are of high quality — fighters tested them out last year at a training area in Kyiv. Not a single bullet penetrated the Estonian plates. The bloodstained body armour won't be seeing retirement any time soon; it will continue on serving Gunya.

Gunya's recovery has been a long process. Several surgeries have been performed on his arm. Metal plates were inserted to connect the bones with one another. A famous medical professor was called to the Rivne hospital where Gunya was being treated. The professor used a unique new method to fill the gap between the injured bones. For this he used bioglass. Gunya's classmates collected money to pay for the bioglass. They managed to collect 20,000 hryvnia. The glass was purchased, and the bones began to grow together.

Bullets don't just damage the body; they also affect the psyche. During the first few weeks after the incident, Gunya was constantly haunted by the two Russian soldiers. As soon as he closed his eyes, their profiles and faces appeared before him. "For two weeks, the mugs of those Russians were in front of my eyes," says Gunya. "One was taller, with a tanned complexion, a black beard, and black hair. The other had light hair and was shorter. Anyway, it's better that their faces are on my mind. Not the other way around."

"Do you believe in God?" I ask. "Of course," Gunya replies. And he retrieves a worn booklet titled *A Fighter's Spiritual Body Armor*. It contains various prayers, including prayers for before battle, for the front lines, and a commander's prayer. There's also a prayer for the enemy. "Have you ever prayed for the enemy?" I ask. "I might have even," responds Gunya.

Where does the pseudonym Gunya originate from? When Andrei was little, he didn't start speaking at a very early age. Even at the age of two, he sometimes spoke a language only he could understand, which sounded like "gu-gu-gu." His mother started calling him Gunya. And Gunya brought that name with him when he joined the battalion. That's the kind of guy Gunya is.

Rubin's Remains From Izyum Forest

In September 2022, I noticed the following ad on social media. They weren't looking for the living. The militants were looking for Sergei, who was also called "The Russian". His *real* nickname was actually "Rubin".

Please help find the body of The Russian. The situation is as follows. The Kharkiv direction is currently in very difficult condition. There are a lot of bodies in the area. A lot of the land has been mined. Searching is difficult: the body could be in a morgue, a basement, a mined building, could be buried, could be on the street, or may even be somewhere outside the Kharkiv area.

Sergei was killed on September 6 near the village of Spivavivka in the Izyum region. He was 35, had a prosthetic starting from his knee on his left leg. Two tattoos on his chest. Wearing an OUN uniform. Probably died from a bullet. If anyone has any information about the possible whereabouts of his body – please come forward.

If anyone has seen any information about his body (photo, video, Russian channels) – please come forward.

I met Sergei—Rubin—in May of 202_ in Zhytomyr. There, the Ukrainian volunteer battalion OUN—the Organization of Ukrainian Nationalists—was preparing to go the front lines. Sergei had been fighting for Ukraine since 2014. In 2015, he lost his leg near Pisk in the Pokrovsky District. When the war broke out, he returned to service. He was killed on September 6, 2022.

Gunya, who I wrote about in the previous story, has a lot to say about the fallen Rubin, words from the heart. "If he were still alive, several others who died would still be alive too," says Gunya. Gunya speaks of several other people who knew Rubin well, who were by his side during the last battle. Dym, Shponder, Tsyvak—these are the men's pseudonyms.

Martin, an Estonian volunteer, told me a week ago that he was going to go retrieve Rubin's body with one of the comrades, Tsyvak. Or rather, what's left of his body.

"Done!," Martin tells me over the phone a few days ago. "We found it. Brought it back." He sends me photos taken in the woods near Izyum. One of them shows Rubin's prosthetic leg.

Now that Rubin's remains have been found, his friends called Rubin's mother in St. Petersburg. They tried to call. His mother wouldn't pick up the call from a Ukrainian number. She's not interested in knowing anything about her son.

Rubin is remembered and thought of. He's become a legend. I get Dym's contact info from Gunya. I met Dym and Shponder yesterday. They describe the events of September 6.

A battle in the woods near Izyum. The Russians have the advantage of numbers. Rubin's unit retreats under heavy fire. Rubin is running in front of Shponder. He can't squat and move with his prosthetic leg like the rest of them. He's hit in the back of the neck by an enemy bullet. Tsyvak runs to him. Turns him around. He's dead. There's no way to take him with them at this point. It would mean more deaths. Now, nine months later, Tsyvak and the men of Cargo 200 are doing what they couldn't do then. Bringing Rubin's remains back from under Izyum forest.

Where will Rubin be buried? Don't know. One option is Zaporizhzhia. When Rubin came from Russia to Ukraine in 2014 to defend Ukrainian freedom in the Maidan, he lived at a friend's father's place in Zaporizhzhia. The friend was killed in the war. Maybe Rubin will be buried next to his friend in the Zaporizhzhia cemetery. But that won't be for a while. Before that, a DNA test has to confirm that the remains are really his.

On the day before the fatal retreat, Rubin was different than usual. Quieter, more pensive. So Dym says. Maybe he anticipated his coming demise. I'm looking at a photo taken of Rubin shortly before his death. I see the shadow over his face.

Fireworks in Mariupol and
The Scorched Fields of Yaroslav

I have never witnessed crops burning. What a charred field stretching to the horizon would look like.

I have now, but only through a video and photos. Those were taken by Yaroslav, a farmer from the village of Temyrivka in the Zaporizhzhia Oblast. Temyrivka is actually located at the intersection of three oblasts—Zaporizhzhia, Dnipropetrovsk and Donetsk. It's a region that has suffered greatly in the war.

We couldn't visit the scorched fields and the shattered village in person. Fierce battles are currently raging in the area. Two weeks ago, Yaroslav went to inspect his lands and the ruins of his buildings. The village is nearly deserted, with only about fifteen people left in it. There are no Ukrainian troops in the village, yet the Russians continue to bomb it. Yaroslav mentions that one shell used to destroy houses costs more than the houses themselves. During his stay in the village, a Russian drone flew over it. A drone-guided artillery barrage followed. Later, Yaroslav found the video footage of the same drone on a Telegram channel. It had dramatic music over it and a narrator's voice boasting about how much damage was done to Ukrainian forces in the village that day.

Yaroslav, aged forty-four, was born in the Donetsk Oblast. He moved to the Zaporizhzhia region in 2002. He studied metallurgy and financial management at university. Worked. Got married. Twelve years ago took over a farm that belonged to his wife's parents. He built it up. It includes 4,000 hectares of farmland. He cultivates grains, sunflowers, and alfalfa. Grains were primarily exported to Africa through Berdiansk Port. Animal feed went to Italy. This very large farm has a fitting name, inherited from the days when it was formerly a collective farm. The collective was called MIR (meaning 'world' or 'peace') and the farm now bears the same name. The land belongs to local villagers and the company rents it from them. MIR was the largest employer in the village.

In the spring of 2022, the village lost its electricity. With the help of generators, Yaroslav tried to keep production going. On April 18, 2022, the village and all farm buildings came under heavy Russian fire. Everything that could burn did. A warehouse containing 2,000 tons of sunflower seeds was destroyed. Before the war, a ton of sunflower seeds was worth 800 USD, and a ton of wheat 350 USD. The sunflower seed warehouse burned for two weeks. The wheat warehouse burned down. What remained was spoiled from rainwater pouring down through the damaged roof. The whole lot of it. The remnants of the crops are still fermenting and rotting to this day.

The primary time for selling the harvest has always been March. The harvest of 2021 should have been sold in 2022. It was never sold, instead destroyed. The winter wheat sown at the end of 2021 was waiting to be harvested in the summer of 2022. It wasn't harvested. The crops burned in the fields. At certain periods the fields were subjected to thirty Grad rocket strikes per hour. One thousand five hundred hectares of wheat fields burned.

Yaroslav estimates the damage at 250 million hryvnia. That's approximately six million euros. This is without including the expenses for the restoring of buildings and fields or the clearing of unexploded ordnance.

"We will definitely rebuild everything," says Yaroslav. They haven't thought for a moment of giving up. The war has reshaped values. Yaroslav isn't afraid of restoring the farm. He's afraid of the war. When the destruction of the village began, Yaroslav felt powerless. It was as if the ground had disappeared from under his feet. Now, he can even find moments of joy, he says.

Yaroslav's company built a church in the village before the war. It too, has been destroyed. It will have to be rebuilt. The church now in ruins was even under the jurisdiction of the Moscow Patriarchate. The new one will be under the Ukrainian Orthodox Church, smiles Yaroslav.

He already sent his wife and child to Canada during the previous year. Maybe what's happening is the third world war, ponders Yaroslav. It's just taking place in Ukraine.

Yaroslav's sister, Tamara, lived in Mariupol with her family. Last spring, they managed to leave for Zaporizhzhia. I meet Tamara, her husband Oleg, and their young daughter Leta.

Tamara

Listening to Tamara and Oleg's story, I feel incredibly weary. I've met dozens of people who've experienced the horrors of Mariupol. I look at myself from a distance and I'm shocked that their story doesn't faze me. That's because there's so much in common among all these people's memories of what happened. I've heard it all so many times. But unlike me, they lived through it all on their own, in their real lives. I didn't. I just listen and write stories. They didn't write about their story in Mariupol, nor did they think about recounting it. They lived and survived—those who I've had the chance to meet. They endured horrendous times that will stay with them forever. While moving through the city under shelling and mines, they tried to find something to eat from warehouses that had already been broken into and looted. They wrapped their children in blankets in freezing basements. Stood in line as the five-hundredth person waiting for water at the well, hurled themselves to the ground as Grad rockets rained down, and witnessed people dying beside them. They saw corpses and human body parts lying in the streets. Dogs who would chew on those remains.

Do you know what the Russian word *фейерверк* means? It's fireworks. Three-year-old Leta was only two during a time of terrible shelling. A couple of months earlier, it was New Year's Eve 2022. Everywhere in Ukraine, including Mariupol, there were fireworks, *фейерверк*. When the Russians started destroying the city and killing its residents at the end of February, Leta thought it was just fireworks. Her parents didn't try to convince her otherwise. They believe that this belief saved Leta from deeper traumas.

On March 18, Tamara's family managed to join a convoy of cars fleeing the city. They did this in the belief and hope that the Russians wouldn't shoot at a convoy. Naive people. Of course, they did. They just got lucky this time. When you have to go, you have to go. A woman in the middle of the convoy stopped her car and went out to pee. No one could get past her. The surroundings of the roads were mined. The risk remained. A stationary convoy is an easy target. This time it went so that the woman finished peeing and everyone could continue on driving.

Tamara is eleven years younger than Yaroslav. When her brother moved away from home and went off to study, Tamara was still a little girl. When Yaroslav came home to visit, he brought his sister a rubber toy. Once, he brought her soft, light-blue dog-shaped slippers. That she remembers.

An Hour With a Prostitute

In a Ukrainian town near the front—a depressing small town in my eyes—lives and works Ruslana. Ruslana's a prostitute. Her nickname is "Lysicha"—"Fox". She doesn't work in a brothel, she doesn't get hassled by mafiosos or bossed around by pimps. Ruslana is an independent business woman. You could say—an independent contractor. The cops sometimes hassle her. Put her in their car, take her somewhere. Let her go later. You can always reach an agreement with them.

Ruslana finds her clients on the small town's dusty centre street. She stands there, wearing tight-fitting shorts with lace trim. Traffic is heavy here. Cars stop. Exchanges are made. Buying and selling. Twice a month, before and after her menstruation, Ruslana visits the doctor to check whether she's caught any disease. Ruslana's sister is a medic by profession. The sister is the head of the town morgue. Ruslana can also ask her sister for health advice if need be.

Somewhere, Ruslana's years of employment are being tallied, and when the time comes, she'll start getting a bit of a pension from the state. It won't be for a while. Ruslana is forty-one years old and does not yet intend to retire. Ruslana is a mother. Her fifteen-year-old son lives in Dnipro. Does your son know? "I don't know if he knows," Ruslana answers.

I spend an hour with Ruslana, and pay shamefully little for it. Just two hundred hryvnia. That's five euros. Ruslana doesn't have a fixed fee. She charges regular customers less. The average tariff is one thousand six hundred hryvnia per session. She charges me so little because I just want to have a chat with her in the back of the fixer's car. That's all. Ruslana is a phenomenal storyteller. With very rich and figurative language. She likes conversing, and does so with pleasure.

War brings a huge number of men together and moves them away from normal life. Women too, but right now we're talking about the men. These men also create a market for prostitution. Where there's demand, there's supply. Of course, prostitutes had work before the war and will have work after it, but war creates more demand for this kind of service in areas close to the front. "99% of my clients are military," says Ruslana.

It's only lunchtime. Today Ruslana has already had three customers. Three soldiers. On a warm summer's day, Ruslana usually does her work concealed behind a spruce hedge in the city park. Most of the revenue comes from oral sex. With two out of three clients today, work was over quickly. The third one was drunk, so with him it was more complicated. Yesterday there were seven clients. On her record day, Ruslana served twelve customers. "That was way too many," she says.

Ruslana doesn't like officers. They tend to be arrogant, make themselves important, flaunt their medals. She sends them straight to... Well, doesn't matter where. The usual client is a soldier, a sergeant or a *starchina*, meaning 'senior'. Mostly Ukrainians, but recently there was an American from a foreign legion. With him, though, the language barrier was an issue.

There are clients who pour their hearts out to Ruslana. Last August, a soldier came to her, whose twelve-year-old daughter had called him. The daughter told her father that mom had gone away with another man. The soldier stayed with Ruslana for the whole day.

Two men have fallen head over heels in love with Ruslana. One is a local driver who divorced his wife for Ruslana. His name is Ruslan. Rusik, as Ruslana calls him. Rusik hopes to live with Ruslana. He keeps confessing his love, says Ruslana. I love you, I love you... It's hard for the guy. Being a driver as he is, he often drives past Ruslana standing on the street. He then stops the car and starts confessing his love...

The second lovesick one is a forty-two-year-old military man from Zaporizhzhia. Serjoga. He fell in love last fall, and now he comes to this small town every chance he gets, to see Ruslana. "When the war ends you'll come with me," Serjoga says.

How many customers has Ruslana had in her lifetime? Ruslana points to a spruce tree nearby. As many as there are thorns on that spruce. She adds, "Instead of thorns, imagine..." well, penises, let's just say. I can imagine. At the age of thirteen, Ruslana lost her virginity to a teacher—a student teacher, to be exact. At the age of fifteen, she started selling herself. Twenty-six continuous years of work experience.

My fixer Sasha, sitting in the front seat, asks if Ruslana ever actually enjoys any of the sex with her clients. Depends on the customer. She had her last orgasm a week ago—with a client.

Clients differ greatly. Some are very strange, with strange requests. One of the top officials of this depressing small town likes this one particular thing. He takes Ruslana to his apartment. Undresses himself. Puts on roller skates. And then has Ruslana hold his penis and pull him around the apartment by it.

Years ago, Ruslana was in a so-called open relationship for a while with a man who is now at war. That open relationship ended after Ruslana went to a party one night. When she came home, the man, who worked as a police officer, put a knife to her throat. It must have been jealousy.

"I'm a person with an average income," says Ruslana. Money ruins a person. One time, when I received a very large sum at once, I felt how it started to change me. I was rude, I insulted people.

The years go by. What will happen when my best before date is up? Then I'll go to lovesick Rusik, says Ruslana. Then I'll let him take care of me.

My hour with Ruslana is up. We take her back to the same place we picked her up from. Ruslana's not in a hurry to get out of the car. She starts asking me questions. What, where, for how long, how many times. Well, that's no longer the subject of this story.

Ruslana steps out. Sasha turns the car around. When I try to spot Ruslana again, she's already gone. A passing car has already picked her up.

Water in Kherson and Afanasiivka

Kherson is currently off limits to journalists. To every rule, however, there is an exception. We manage to enter the city. By "we," I mean my fixer Sasha and I. No, we didn't bribe anyone. We're just lucky like that. We are accompanied by a press officer whose car has broken down. We take him from Mykolaiv to Kherson, and that's how we made it into the city.

The press officer has experience with journalists. He knows what they are looking for. He says that some people get lucky. You take them to the Dnipro River, and behold — a corpse floats by. If only it were an enemy corpse, I think to myself.

We, delighted about having made it into the city, don't see any enemy corpses floating by. We see the river and the flooded area from a distance. We aren't allowed past the guard posts to get to the riverbank. Soldiers tell us that there had just been an enemy reconnaissance drone called Orlan hovering over the city. It's mapping out targets and areas to direct fire. When Orlan is in the air, a larger attack is imminent, say the soldiers. We hear explosions, but not too frequently. We hide behind a stone wall and wait.

Some people have just been brought out of flooded houses in the area by motorboat. I talk to them. They all live in the Ostrov district. Ostrov means 'island', but it's not really an island. It's a peninsula that extends into the river. Which has now been flooded by the river. I ask, I talk, I listen. But I feel anxious about not having been on the boat that brought them out. That I didn't get to see them climbing into the boat through their windows. That I didn't get to see an enemy corpse float by.

Konstantin

Konstantin is a tired, sixty-seven-year-old man. He's holding two plastic bags filled with food he brought along from his home in Ostrov. In the bag you can see a couple of loaves of bread, a can of fish, a bottle of ketchup, and some oatmeal. Konstantin stands there, looking dazed and confused. He doesn't want to go anywhere. He just wants to wait for the water to recede so he can go back home.

I inquire about his life. Konstantin is a man with a higher education in technology, who worked as a shipwright at the Kherson shipbuilding plant for many years. He had a job and a family. Three years ago, his wife and daughter left—to Kamchatka. His wife was from there. I ask if his wife was pro-Ukrainian or pro-Russian. "Sort of both," he replies. That's a strange answer. Just like saying someone's "sort of pregnant".

Konstantin has a summer cottage on the left bank of the river, which is under Russian occupation. It's currently completely underwater. As I leave, he remains seated on a bench, frozen, waiting for his fate.

Sasha communicates with volunteers who have a narrow, flat-bottomed boat attached to their car on a trailer. They are heading to a village in Kherson Oblast that has become an island. Kalinovka is the name of the village. We join them. We want to reach the village that has become an island. To talk to the remaining people and to deliver the hundreds of bottles of drinking water that we have packed into our car.

After driving for an hour and a half, we reach a point where the small asphalt road leads into the water. Here we could easily lower the motorboat in and head for the village. However, it's too far from here. Seventeen kilometres, which would need to be travelled back and forth multiple times, in order to deliver aid and to transport people. The boat is small and we are many.

I speak with a Ukrainian man there, who travels around with Reuters journalists. He tells me about another village that has also turned into an island, one that is easier to reach. Afanasiivka is located ten kilometres away. Sasha and I leave the volunteers to their plan-making and set out to find Afanasiivka village.

Afanasiivka

From a distance and from a higher vantage point, the village looks like a picturesque island. If only there weren't houses standing half-submerged in water along its shores. By the road leading to the village, which eventually disappears into the water, sits Maria Vassilyevna, tending to three cows. Two of the cows, Ryabukha and Julia, belong to her. The third one, Malvina, is the neighbour's cow. Maria's home is on the other side of the water in Afanasiivka. This is the fourth day she has been away from home with her cows. She's been living in a former tractor station, waiting for the water to recede so she can return home with Ryabukha, Julia, and Malvina. So she could get back to her normal life. She sells milk in plastic bottles at the town market in nearby Snihurivka. She still has her home — the floodwater reached her garden, but her house remained dry.

Volunteers are a free-spirited and kind-hearted bunch. They help us and our bottles of water reach the flooded village with their inflatable motorboat. To our right there's a stadium — you can see the upper parts of the goalposts poking out of the water. It's currently the perfect place for water polo. A traffic sign barely poking out of the water tells us we're on the main road. As if you could even see any side roads.

Most of the villagers have gathered to a spot where the asphalt road emerges from the water, where the boats bringing aid dock. You could call it a harbour. Aid packages are piled up on a patch of dry land. The village head is probably the woman who's in charge of the distribution. Many people have gathered around her. Not everyone seems satisfied with the principles of distribution. Anxious cries, on the verge of turning into a shouting match, can be heard. The patch gradually empties of aid and of people.

Olga

Seventy-year-old Olga doesn't shout. She waits silently, and is content with what she receives. If only someone would help transport the aid packages to the other side of the village. During the peak of the flood, Olga's house was submerged up to the chimney. Now the water has slightly receded. What kind of scene awaits her when the water finally recedes completely? Everything, all her worldly possessions, were submerged underwater. Home appliances, furniture, mementos, clothing — all of it. She managed to take her dogs, cats, and documents with her when the water began rising. Olga has been and continues to live alone. Her only son was killed by his "friends" during a drinking binge eight years ago. Alyosha was thirty-six at the time, and that's how old he'll remain. He left three children behind. Olga starts to cry. As I leave, Olga is still waiting for someone to help transport the aid packages to her submerged home. She's staying with her neighbour for now.

Ludmilla

Fifty-one-year-old Ludmilla got married at a young age and her husband brought her to Afanasiivka. Ludmilla has been living here for thirty-two years. Her two daughters have married and have had children of their own. During the occupation, her daughter came from Snihurivka to live with her, along with her ten-year-old daughter, Yevgenia. "After eight months of occupation, Zhenya has become an adult," says Ludmilla. "How serious she has become. I always sat with her as she was falling asleep. Zhenya held my hand tightly. When I took my arm away, she would wake up."

"Everything is destroyed," Ludmilla says while standing knee-deep in water in front of her home. "There were thirty-five rose bushes in the garden. Two of my cows are wandering around the village. The chickens are being kept by my neighbor. I'm like a bum, an outcast..." Now there's an abundance of water in this village. An abundance of watery eyes as well. Ludmilla cries.

Aleksander

Aleksander, on his green bicycle, approaches me himself, stops and strikes up a conversation. Aleksander is a bridge builder and his calling seems to be the building of spiritual bridges as well. Forty-three-year-old Aleksander is open and honest. The kind of person you, for some reason, just instantly warm up to.

I ask him about what the occupiers did in the village during their eight month long presence there. Aleksander tells me about Anatoly, who was seventy.

Russian soldiers entered Anatoly's house and asked for something to drink. "What are you doing here? Go away," Anatoly told them. "I'm not giving you any water. Nobody here has been waiting for you."

The soldiers took Anatoly with them. He was found dead, with his arms and legs broken.

Water. The things people do for it and with it.

ibidem.eu